How to Use This Book

Look for these special features in this book:

SIDEBARS, **CHARTS**, **GRAPHS**, and original **MAPS** expand your understanding of what's being discussed—and also make useful sources for classroom reports.

FAQs answer common **F**requently **A**sked **Q**uestions about people, places, and things.

WOW FACTORS offer "Who knew?" facts to keep you thinking.

TRAVEL GUIDE gives you tips on exploring the state—either in person or right from your chair!

PROJECT ROOM provides fun ideas for school assignments and incredible research projects. Plus, there's a guide to primary sources—what they are and how to cite them.

Please note: All statistics are as up-to-date as possible at the time of publication.

Consultants: W. Jeffrey Bolster, Associate Professor of History, University of New Hampshire; William Loren Katz; Peter Thompson, Professor of Geology, University of New Hampshire

Book production by The Design Lab

Library of Congress Cataloging-in-Publication Data

Kent, Deborah.
 New Hampshire / Deborah Kent.
    p. cm.—(America the beautiful. Third series)
 Includes bibliographical references and index.
 ISBN-13: 978-0-531-18501-8
 ISBN-10: 0-531-18501-X
 1. New Hampshire—Juvenile literature. I. Title. II. Series.
 F34.3.K46 2009
 974.2—dc22   2008048940

1 2 3 4 5 6 7 8 9 10 R 19 18 17 16 15 14 13 12 11 10

AMERICA ★ THE ★ BEAUTIFUL

New Hampshire

BY DEBORAH KENT

Third Series

Children's Press®
An Imprint of Scholastic Inc.
New York ★ Toronto ★ London ★ Auckland ★ Sydney
Mexico City ★ New Delhi ★ Hong Kong
Danbury, Connecticut

CONTENTS

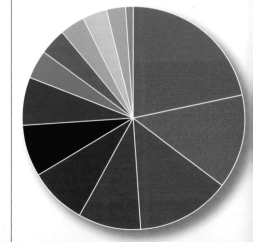

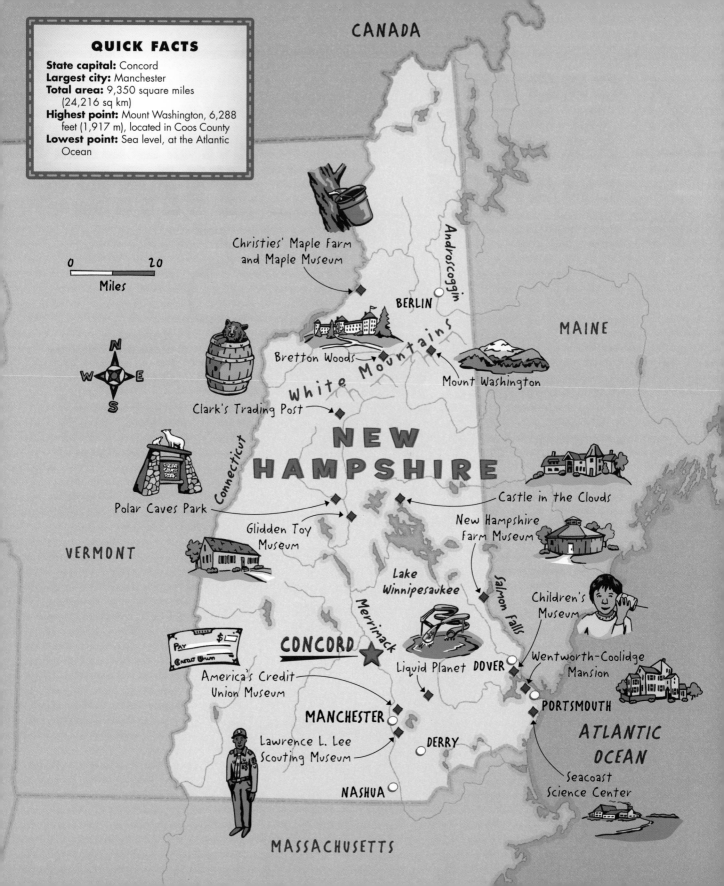

CANADA

QUICK FACTS

State capital: Concord
Largest city: Manchester
Total area: 9,350 square miles
  (24,216 sq km)
Highest point: Mount Washington, 6,288
  feet (1,917 m), located in Coos County
Lowest point: Sea level, at the Atlantic
  Ocean

Christies' Maple Farm
and Maple Museum

Androscoggin

0   20
Miles

BERLIN

MAINE

N
W · E
S

Bretton Woods

White Mountains

Mount Washington

Clark's Trading Post

NEW
HAMPSHIRE

Polar Caves Park

Connecticut

Castle in the Clouds

New Hampshire
Farm Museum

VERMONT

Glidden Toy
Museum

Lake
Winnipesaukee

Salmon Falls

Children's
Museum

Wentworth-Coolidge
Mansion

Merrimack

CONCORD

PAY
$
Credit Union

America's Credit
Union Museum

Liquid Planet

DOVER

PORTSMOUTH

ATLANTIC
OCEAN

MANCHESTER

Lawrence L. Lee
Scouting Museum

DERRY

Seacoast
Science Center

NASHUA

MASSACHUSETTS

Welcome to New Hampshire!

HOW DID NEW HAMPSHIRE GET ITS NAME?

In the early 1600s, England claimed the region known as New England in what is now the northeastern United States. In 1620, King James I met with officials from a company called the Plymouth Council for New England. He gave the company permission to hand out grants of land to businesspeople and settlers. The council gave a large piece of land in northern New England to two businessmen, Ferdinando Gorges and John Mason. Gorges and Mason divided this property in 1629. Mason's land lay between the Merrimack and Piscataqua rivers. He named this land New Hampshire, after the English county of Hampshire where he grew up. John Mason never set foot in New Hampshire, but nearly 400 years later it still carries the name he chose.

NEW HAMPSHIRE→

ATLANTIC OCEAN

8

READ ABOUT

A stream flows through the granite rocks of the White Mountains.

C H A P T E R   O N E

LAND

★

"IN NEW HAMPSHIRE," WRITES HOWARD MANSFIELD OF HANCOCK, "STONE— GRANITE—IS WHAT WE HAVE. We have lakes and mountains and five or six seasons of weather, but mostly what we have is granite." New Hampshire's granite and its other rock give the state a wild beauty, shaping its lakes, seacoast, and mountains. From the state's high point of 6,288 feet (1,917 meters) at Mount Washington to its low point at sea level along the coast, New Hampshire's 9,350 square miles (24,216 square kilometers) are a feast for the senses.

Snow covers the Windsor-Cornish Bridge, which crosses the Connecticut River along the New Hampshire-Vermont border.

FAQ

Q8 WHICH STATES ARE SMALLER THAN NEW HAMPSHIRE?

A8 The four states smaller than New Hampshire are New Jersey, Connecticut, Delaware, and Rhode Island.

THE LAY OF THE LAND

New Hampshire ranks 46th in size among the states. At its greatest length, New Hampshire stretches 180 miles (290 km) from north to south. At its widest point, it measures 93 miles (150 km) across.

New Hampshire is one of the six New England states (the others are Maine, Vermont, Massachusetts, Rhode Island, and Connecticut). On a map, New Hampshire looks like a tall, narrow triangle with one ragged side. In the far northwest and at its northern tip, it shares a border with the Canadian province of Quebec. A razor-straight line forms most of its eastern border with Maine. The border with Massachusetts to the south is also straight, except for one uneven corner at the eastern end. The curves of the Connecticut River, which form the long, ragged western side of the triangle, separate New Hampshire from Vermont.

New Hampshire Topography

Use the color-coded elevation chart to see on the map New Hampshire's high points (red to orange) and low points (green). Elevation is measured as the distance above or below sea level.

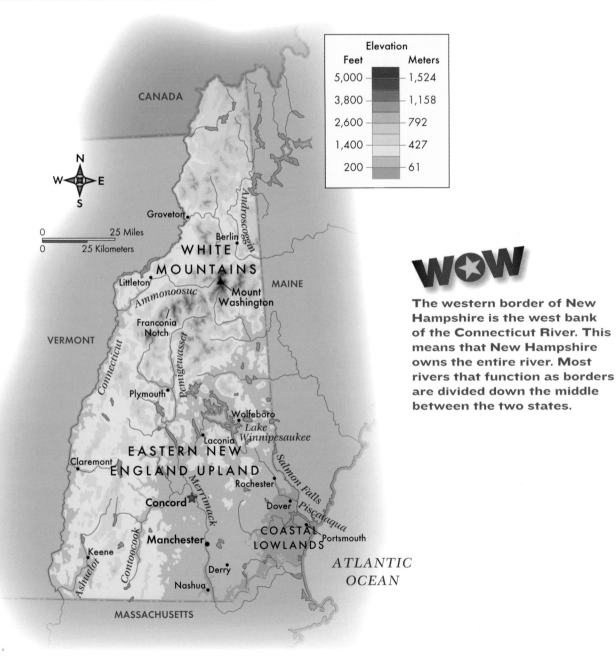

Elevation	
Feet	Meters
5,000	1,524
3,800	1,158
2,600	792
1,400	427
200	61

WOW

The western border of New Hampshire is the west bank of the **Connecticut River**. This means that New Hampshire owns the entire river. Most rivers that function as borders are divided down the middle between the two states.

New Hampshire Geo-Facts

Along with the state's geographical highlights, this chart ranks New Hampshire's land, water, and total area compared to all other states.

Total area; rank	9,350 square miles (24,216 sq km); 46th
Land; rank	8,968 square miles (23,227 sq km); 44th
Water; rank	382 square miles (989 sq km); 45th
Inland water; rank	314 square miles (813 sq km); 44th
Territorial water; rank	68 square miles (176 sq km); 22nd
Geographic center	Belknap, 3 miles (5 km) east of Ashland
Latitude	42°40' N to 45°18' N
Longitude	70°37' W to 72°37' W
Highest point	Mount Washington, 6,288 feet (1,917 m), located in Coos County
Lowest point	Sea level, at the Atlantic Ocean
Largest city	Manchester
Longest river	Connecticut

Source: U.S. Census Bureau

 **Tiny New Hampshire could fit into Alaska, the largest state, almost 71 times!**

WORD TO KNOW

metamorphic *describing rocks that have been changed by extreme pressure, wind, and water*

ROCKS AND ICE

Although New Hampshire is called the Granite State, less than half the rock that underlies it is granite. Granite is a very hard rock that forms from rock that has cooled and hardened. Most of the rest is made of **metamorphic** rocks. These are rocks that were changed from the original mudstone and sandstone owing to immense heat and pressure deep underground. The Presidential Range in the White Mountains, for example, is metamorphic.

This metamorphic rock formed about 400 million years ago, before the age of the dinosaurs, when New Hampshire collided with Vermont. The rocks we see today at the surface were once under the much taller Appalachian Mountains. Imagine how much rock has been eroded and washed to the sea in that much time!

Some of the granite in New Hampshire formed when the metamorphic rocks became so hot that they began to melt and later turned into granite. Other granite formed from melted rock in magma chambers, large pools of molten rock beneath ancient volcanoes such as the Ossipee Mountains and the Franconia Range.

A series of glaciers helped shape New Hampshire, beginning about 50,000 years ago. Immense sheets of ice ground slowly from the north, crushing boulders,

Hikers on top of Mount Monadnock

gouging holes, and pushing walls of rubble before them. The last glacier reached as far south as central New Jersey. By the time it receded, about 12,000 years ago, it had carved hundreds of lakes and valleys in what is now New Hampshire. It left heaps of boulders and broken rock that eventually became hills. Deposits of finely ground stone became rich soil where forests took root.

Clear traces of the last glacier can still be seen in New Hampshire. In some places, the glacier left fields of rounded, protruding rocks. In other places, rivers flowing under the ice left narrow ridges made of sand and gravel, called **eskers**. Shallow grooves on the top of Mount Kearsarge and other New Hampshire mountains show where the moving ice dragged rocks toward the southeast. New Hampshire has several **monadnocks**, mountains that stand alone because they are made of hard, resistant rock that did not wear down when the rocks around them eroded away.

Monadnock, a term used around the world, is named for Monadnock Mountain in Cheshire County, New Hampshire.

WORDS TO KNOW

eskers *fields of jagged, protruding rocks*

monadnocks *giant outcrops of rock that did not wear away as surrounding rock was ground down*

A tour boat passes by Lunging Island.

New Hampshire has the shortest coastline of any coastal state, only 18 miles (29 km) in all!

WORD TO KNOW

brackish *slightly salty*

LAND REGIONS

The geography of New Hampshire can be divided into three main land regions. They are the Coastal Lowlands, the New England Upland, and the White Mountains Region.

The Coastal Lowlands

The southeastern corner of New Hampshire belongs to the Coastal Lowlands region. This region is part of a long, narrow plain that extends from New England to Florida. Several small rivers empty into Great Bay, which empties into the ocean by way of the Piscataqua River, a **brackish** inlet that winds across the lowlands. About 9 miles (14 km) offshore lie a group of islands called the Isles of

Shoals. The three southern islands—Star Island, White Island, and Lunging Island—belong to New Hampshire. The islands to the north are part of Maine.

The New England Upland

Most of central and southern New Hampshire falls into the region called the New England Upland. This region extends from northern Maine to eastern Connecticut. In New Hampshire, it includes the Merrimack River valley and the Connecticut River valley, as well as an area known as the Hills and Lakes Region. The Connecticut River valley is a narrow, fertile strip of land following the river's 211-mile (340 km) course along New Hampshire's western edge. The Merrimack Valley reaches north from the Massachusetts border into the middle of the state. The Hills and Lakes Region includes many scenic lakes. The largest and best known is Lake Winnipesaukee.

The White Mountains Region

The White Mountains stretch across northern New Hampshire. They are steep, rugged, rocky mountains with many swift streams. The White Mountains are part of the Appalachian mountain chain that stretches from Maine to Georgia. Several ranges make up the White Mountains group. The best known is the Presidential Range, which includes the tallest peaks in New England. Five peaks in this range are named for the first five U.S. presidents: Washington, Adams, Jefferson, Madison, and Monroe. Because of the harsh climate, no trees grow on the peaks of these mountains. Instead, they are topped with barren rock. Glaciers carved deep, scenic notches in the White Mountains, including Franconia Notch and Crawford Notch.

THE END OF AN EMBLEM

In 1805, several New Hampshirites discovered a strange rock formation on Profile Mountain, which overlooks Franconia Notch. Standing 40 feet (12 m) high and 25 feet (8 m) wide, the formation looked very much like a human face. "The Old Man of the Mountain" became New Hampshire's beloved state symbol. Generations of visitors gazed up at it, and it "gazed" back. On May 3, 2003, weakened by thousands of years of water freezing in its cracks, the great stone face suddenly collapsed and tumbled down the mountainside.

Mount Washington is the tallest peak in the northeastern United States.

Weather Report

This chart shows record temperatures (high and low) for the state, as well as average temperatures (July and January) and average annual precipitation.

Record high temperature . . . . 106°F (41°C) at Nashua
on July 4, 1911
Record low temperature . . . −47°F (−44°C) at Mount Washington
on January 29, 1934
Average July temperature .71°F (22°C)
Average January temperature . . . . 23°F (−5°C)
Average yearly precipitation . . . . .37 inches (94 cm)

Source: National Climatic Data Center, NESDIS, NOAA, U.S. Department of Commerce

WORD TO KNOW

precipitation *all water that falls to the earth, including rain, sleet, hail, snow, dew, fog, or mist*

On April 12, 1934, instruments at the Mount Washington Observatory measured winds at 231 miles per hour (372 kph). This is the highest wind speed ever measured on land anywhere on Earth!

CLIMATE

In general, New Hampshire has cool summers and frigid winters. Temperatures in the far north are usually about 10 degrees Fahrenheit (5.6 degrees Celsius) lower than those along the border with Massachusetts.

New Hampshire receives about 37 inches (94 centimeters) of **precipitation** a year, in the form of rain, sleet, and snow. Snowfall is lightest along the coast and heaviest in the west and the far north. New Hampshire residents still tell stories of the February 1978 blizzard that kept some families snowbound for up to a week.

Mount Washington has some of the most extreme weather in the world. The peak is often hidden by clouds or fog and is subject to frigid temperatures. Storm systems from the Gulf of Mexico and winds from the west converge at this high point. Since 1932, scientists at the Mount Washington Observatory have been studying the mountain's extreme weather conditions.

The Presidential Range in autumn

PLANT LIFE

The glorious oranges, reds, and yellows of New Hampshire's autumn leaves draw visitors, known as leaf peepers, from far and wide. As the leaves of oaks, maples, beeches, ashes, and birches in the Merrimack Valley change color, the summer woods become an autumn festival.

New Hampshire is one of the most heavily forested states in the nation. Nearly seven-eighths of the state is blanketed with hardwood and evergreen trees. Evergreens such as pine, spruce, hemlock, and cedar grow most thickly in the White Mountains Region.

Blueberry bushes thrive in the acidic soils of New Hampshire's wetlands, stony hills, and mountaintops. In spring, wildflowers such as trout lilies, trilliums, bloodroots, and lady's slippers brighten the woods. Among the gems of the woodland is the purple lilac, New Hampshire's state flower. Daisies and black-eyed Susans splash color across meadows in the summer.

Purple lilac

New Hampshire National Park Areas

This map shows some of New Hampshire's national parks and other areas protected by the National Park Service.

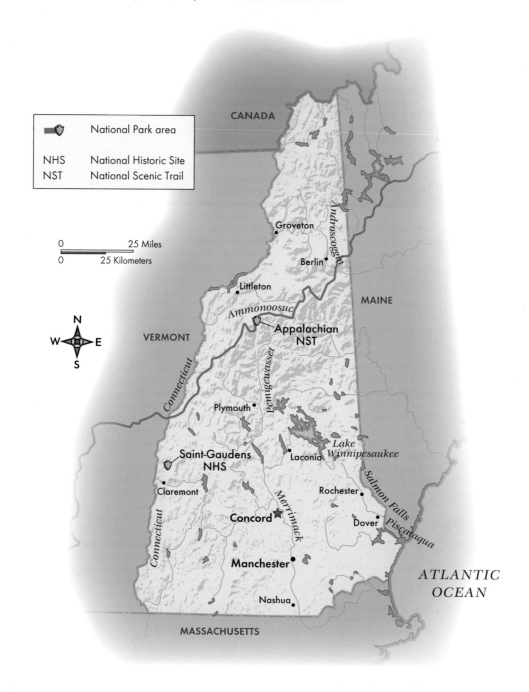

A great blue heron in its nest near Great Bay in Durham

ANIMAL LIFE

Each spring, residents of Manchester, New Hampshire, welcome the return of a pair of peregrine falcons. Since 2001, the birds have nested on a window ledge on a downtown high-rise. Tiny cameras in the nest box send video images of the parents and nestlings to thousands of viewers online.

New Hampshire is home to bird species ranging from bald eagles and peregrine falcons to many kinds of warblers and finches. The lively purple finch with its delicate, melodious song is New Hampshire's state bird. Mallards and herons nest on lakeshores and riverbanks. Each summer, colonies of terns and other shorebirds gather on the Isles of Shoals.

White-tailed deer browse New Hampshire's woods and graze its fields. Bears and moose have made a comeback in recent decades throughout the state.

THINK ABOUT IT!

Taking Care of the Salmon

In the early 1800s, thousands of Atlantic salmon swam up New Hampshire's rivers each spring to lay their eggs. But by the 1890s, overfishing, the damming of streams, and pollution from logging had drastically reduced their numbers. Today, wildlife experts are trying to stock New Hampshire's rivers with salmon raised in fish hatcheries. So far, these efforts have had little success. "We have a moral obligation in one way, since we so clearly wiped them out," said Matt Carpenter, a biologist with the New Hampshire Fish and Game Departmentin 2008. "The **anadromous fish** are struggling right now, and we are really trying to figure out why."

WORD TO KNOW

anadromous fish *fish that spend most of their lives in salt water but breed in freshwater*

Canada lynx, bobcats, and American martens live in the northern woods, seldom seen by humans. Skunks, beavers, opossums, raccoons, and bats often live near towns as well as in wild areas. Opossums have moved into New Hampshire from states to the south.

CARING FOR THE LAND

In April 2006, New Hampshire passed a law to cut down on mercury and sulfur emissions from coal-burning power plants. Lawmakers recognized that mercury pollution was poisoning fish and birds in the state's lakes and rivers and damaging human health. They understood that sulfur harmed air quality and contributed to asthma and other illnesses. New Hampshire's new law was one of the strictest such regulations in the nation.

Most people in New Hampshire consider the state's lakes, streams, and forests to be precious resources. But people also want automobiles, green lawns, electric power, and all the conveniences of modern life. Like most states, New Hampshire faces serious environmental threats from human activity. Chemical pollution and poorly managed logging and development all cause damage.

Organizations such as the New Hampshire Audubon and Environment New Hampshire work to protect the state's water, air, forests, and beaches. They strive to educate the public about environmental issues. Volunteers from these and other groups guard nesting birds and plant trees and wildflowers. The Society for the Protection of New Hampshire Forests has long been working to preserve the state's resources. The organization both buys land to protect it from development and helps private landowners preserve it.

Karner blue butterfly

MINI-BIO

DAVID CARROLL: BIOLOGIST, WRITER, AND ARTIST

From the time he was a boy, David M. Carroll (1940—) of Warner loved to explore swamps and marshes. As a biologist, writer, and artist, he has focused on understanding and preserving New England's wetlands. Carroll is especially interested in freshwater turtles, whose survival is threatened. His books include Trout Reflections, Swampwalker's Journal, and Self-Portrait with Turtles. He has won many awards for his art and nature writing.

? Want to know more? See Self-Portrait with Turtles: A Memoir (New York: Mariner Books, 2005).

NEW HAMPSHIRE'S ENDANGERED SPECIES

Several species in New Hampshire are in danger of becoming extinct. These include the leatherback sea turtle, the eastern puma or cougar, and plants such as the northeastern bulrush, Jesup's milk vetch, and Robbins' cinquefoil.

The Karner blue, New Hampshire's state butterfly, lives on the leaves of the lupine, a wild shrub that grows in pine barrens. Pine barrens are regions of small pines where the soil is generally poor. During the 1980s, developers cleared the pine barrens around Concord to make way for houses and shopping malls. By 2000, the Karner blue butterfly had completely disappeared from New Hampshire. New Hampshire Audubon went into action. The group encouraged New Hampshirites to plant lupine in their gardens, and released Karner blue caterpillars into the area. Within two years, the butterflies were again breeding in the Granite State.

READ ABOUT

Researchers dig
at an ancient site
in Colebrook.

8000 BCE

*The first people enter
present-day New
Hampshire*

▲ **7500 BCE**
*People live at the Smyth
Site, near today's
Manchester*

5000 BCE

*The climate warms, and
forests grow*

CHAPTER TWO

FIRST PEOPLE

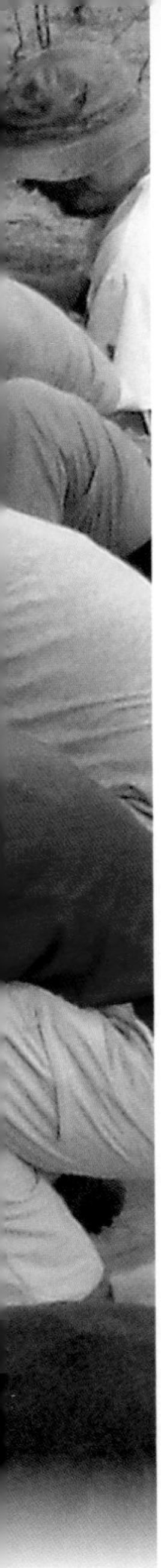

★

IN 1966, THERE WERE PLANS TO IMPROVE THE AMOSKEAG BRIDGE ON THE MERRIMACK RIVER. Construction would destroy a high bluff overlooking the river, a place where early peoples had once made their homes. Before the work got under way, researchers spent more than two years digging at the bluff, known as the Smyth Site. They found traces of human beings who lived there more than 9,000 years ago.

Remains of a
Woodland pot

1000 BCE ▲
People live in settled
villages, beginning the
Woodland Period

Late 1500s CE
*Several Native groups
come together to form the
Pennacook Nation*

1616–1619
*An epidemic kills more
than 90 percent of the
Native people in what is
now New Hampshire*

WORD TO KNOW

tundra *treeless plain*

Atlatl

HUNTERS ON THE TUNDRA

Most archaeologists think that people first entered present-day New Hampshire around 10,000 years ago. By then, the last of the great glaciers had begun to recede. The moving ice left the land a **tundra**. Bands of hunters came to New Hampshire as they followed herds of musk ox, mammoths, and other large game animals. These people were the descendants of nomadic hunters who had crossed into North America from Asia thousands of years earlier.

The hunters used spears tipped with grooved stone points. Similar spearheads, which are called Clovis points after the site in New Mexico where some examples were discovered, have been found across most of North America. As the centuries passed, North American hunters began to use a forked stick called an atlatl to help them throw spears great distances.

ARCHAIC AND WOODLAND PEOPLES

Eventually, the large game animals disappeared, perhaps driven to extinction by human hunters. About 7,000 years ago, the climate started to grow warmer. Thick forests sprang up and covered the once-barren ground. Deer, moose, bears, and other game were plentiful, and the lakes and streams teemed with fish. New Hampshire entered the era archaeologists call the Archaic Period.

During the Archaic Period, people learned to use a variety of new tools and weapons. Stone scrapers, knives, hammers, and ax heads have been found at sites in New Hampshire. People stopped using Clovis points and developed several new kinds of spear tips. Besides hunting, Archaic people fished and gathered edible roots and berries.

A Woodland hunter brings a deer home to his family.

Skeletons from the Archaic Period show that these people were tall, strong, and healthy. Both men and women had muscular arms and legs. They had good teeth and strong bones, suggesting that they enjoyed a nutritious diet.

Sometime around 1000 BCE, northern New England entered the era known as the Woodland Period. By this time, people had learned to make pottery, using clay from the banks of streams and lakes. Bows and arrows replaced hunting spears. The Woodland people planted crops such as corn, squash, and beans. Instead of moving from place to place, they lived for much of the year in settled villages.

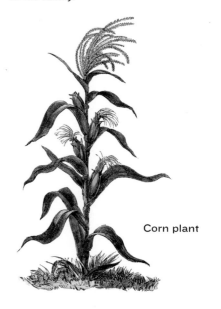

Corn plant

An Algonquian hunter pursues a moose from a birch bark canoe.

WESTERN ABENAKIS

By 1600 CE, many small groups of Native people lived in what is now New Hampshire. Sometimes a powerful leader gathered several groups together in an alliance for defense and trade. In the late 1500s, several groups came together to form the Pennacook Nation.

The Native people of New Hampshire, including the Pennacook people, belonged to a large group of northeastern peoples called the Algonquians. The various Algonquian peoples had similar customs and beliefs and spoke languages with common roots. The Algonquian groups that lived in today's New Hampshire and Vermont are generally known as Western Abenakis. Eastern Abenakis lived in present-day Maine.

The Western Abenaki people consisted of several groups, including Ossipees, Sunapees, Nashuways, and Pennacooks. The Pennacook people were widely respected by neighboring groups because of their power in battle.

Native American Peoples

(Before European Contact)

This map shows the general area of Native American peoples before European settlers arrived.

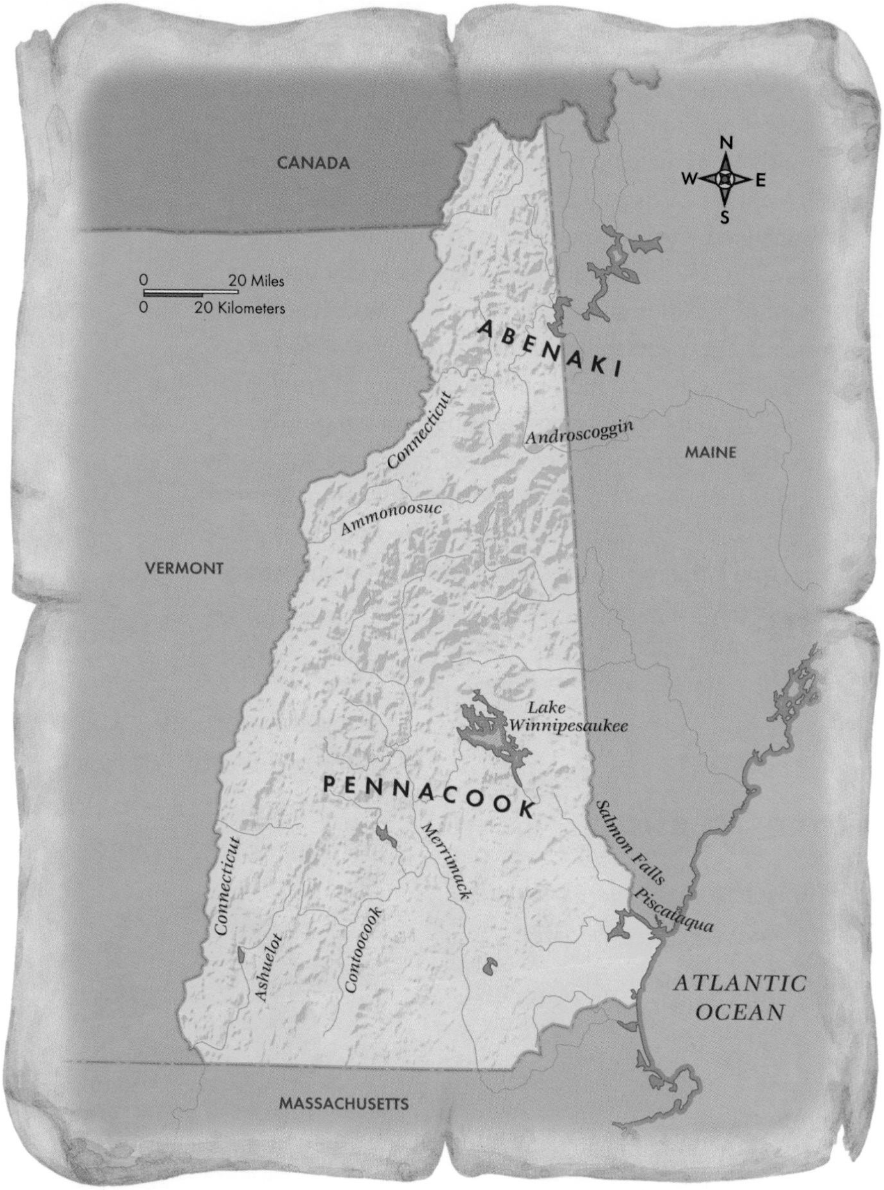

Abenakis often lived in wigwams. They constructed the wigwams by placing poles made from branches or tree trunks in a circle in the ground. The tops were bent toward the center of the circle and tied together with tree bark. Then they covered the poles with mats woven from reeds. Abenakis also built longhouses by tying rows of poles together. A longhouse could be 30 feet (9 m) in length and often housed several families.

Corn was one of their staple foods. Abenakis pounded the corn into meal and then fried or steamed the meal to make corn cakes. Hunters and fighters also carried dried corn in leather pouches. Maple syrup was a special treat among Abenakis. In March, they made holes in the trunks of sugar maple trees and set bowls to catch the

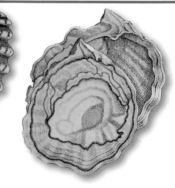

Picture Yourself . . .

Going Clamming

Your mother wakes you and your sister early in the morning, before the first daylight streaks the sky. Quietly you pick up your basket and set out on the long walk to the beach. The brisk morning air helps you feel more awake, and you enjoy the songs of the birds as you pass beneath the trees. When you reach the beach, women and girls from the Agawam band are already there. You don't know their language, but your mother makes friendship signs to them and they smile a welcome. Soon you spot your first clam burrow. You dig down quickly with your stick, pull the clam out of the damp sand, and drop it into your basket. An Agawam girl shows you her basket, already heavy with her morning's catch. She points to a spot below the rocks and shows you that there are many burrows there. Soon you are crouched side by side, digging and laughing. Even without words, you understand each other perfectly.

oozing sap. They boiled the sap to remove water, leaving a pure, sweet syrup.

Although Abenakis grew some of their own food, they also depended on hunting, fishing, and gathering. Men and boys stretched nets across streams to catch fish. They also speared fish, hunted deer and bears with bows and arrows, and set snares for rabbits and other small game. Abenaki women and girls dug clams on the beaches and gathered fruits, berries, and nuts in the woods.

Western Abenakis made their clothing from animal skins. Women wore long deerskin skirts, and men wore leggings in winter and **breechcloths** in warm weather. They made moccasins from deerskin or moose leather. Men sometimes wore long leather stockings that protected them from prickly bushes while they were hunting. Both men and women sometimes wore cloaks of skins draped over their shoulders.

WORD TO KNOW

breechcloths *garments worn by men over their lower bodies*

Moccasins

Abenakis made jewelry from brightly colored stones and pounded copper. They also wore tattoos on their faces. The tattoos depicted birds and animals found in the New England forests.

In autumn, when the crops had been harvested, groups of Abenakis gathered for games and dancing. Men and women did not dance together. Instead, some dances were for men, and others were for women and girls. Men and boys enjoyed juggling contests, wrestling matches, and races.

THE INDIAN FEVER

In 1616, a deadly epidemic suddenly swept the Abenaki villages. People grew feverish and broke out in painful sores. Their skin turned yellow. Few who were stricken ever recovered.

Historians have never identified the disease that struck the Indians of New England. Some experts believe it may have been chicken pox. French and English fishers, sailing along the coast and coming ashore for food and water, may have exposed the Native Americans to the disease.

The Indians had never before encountered chicken pox, measles, and other European illnesses. They had no natural **immunity** against these diseases, and the results were disastrous. Historians estimate that from 90 to 98 percent of Western Abenakis died between 1616 and 1619. By the early 1620s, families and entire villages had been wiped out. Powerful chiefs and warriors had fallen.

Yet another catastrophe awaited the Abenaki people. Pale-skinned strangers would soon settle in New Hampshire and force the Indians to leave the land of their ancestors.

SEE IT HERE!

MOUNT KEARSARGE INDIAN MUSEUM

Would you like to throw a spear using an atlatl? Or learn how Indians long ago made their clothes? You can when you visit the Mount Kearsarge Indian Museum in Warner. The museum strives to teach respect for the land and its early inhabitants. Outside the museum, peaceful trails and gardens of native plants provide a refuge from the hectic pace of modern life.

WORD TO KNOW

immunity *protection against disease*

READ ABOUT

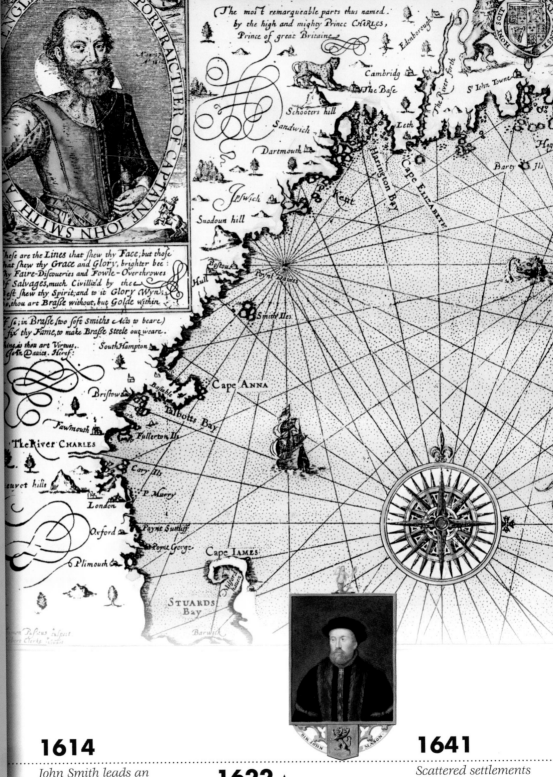

John Smith's map of New England

1614

John Smith leads an expedition up the New England coast and stops at the Isles of Shoals

1622 ▲

John Mason receives a large land grant in what is now New Hampshire

1641

Scattered settlements in present-day New Hampshire join the Massachusetts Bay Colony

CHAPTER THREE

EXPLORATION AND SETTLEMENT

★

IN 1614, ENGLISH ADVENTURER JOHN SMITH SAILED UP THE NEW ENGLAND COAST. He anchored briefly at the Isles of Shoals, which he named the Smith Isles after himself. Smith and other early explorers carried glowing reports of their discoveries back to the English king, James I. They told of vast wildlife and endless forests. They convinced the king that this region could bring riches and power to the English throne.

1691

New Hampshire becomes a separate colony

1754 ▶

Robert Rogers forms Rogers' Rangers to attack the French in Canada

1788 ▶

New Hampshire ratifies the U.S. Constitution, becoming the ninth state.

THE PLYMOUTH COUNCIL FOR NEW ENGLAND

Years earlier, in 1605, French explorer Samuel de Champlain had mapped the coastline. After studying the maps of Smith, Champlain, and other explorers, King James gave the name New England to the region that stretched from today's Maine to Connecticut. He appointed English merchant Sir Ferdinando Gorges to head the Plymouth Council, a group of businessmen, for New England. The council was free to give land in the region to anyone who wanted to develop trade.

In 1622, Gorges and John Mason, the governor of Newfoundland in Canada, received a land grant in today's New Hampshire. Over the next few years, Mason and Gorges received four more grants. The men of the Plymouth Council had never seen North America, and their maps were far from accurate. The boundaries of their land grants were vague at best. No one knew for sure what land belonged to Mason and Gorges, and what belonged to other investors. After a few years, Gorges and Mason divided their land grants. Gorges took the eastern portion, which became the state of Maine. Mason held much of present-day New Hampshire.

Confusion about the boundaries of Mason's land grants went on for years. Legal battles over the claims raged for 150 years!

PANNAWAY

As a clerk with the Plymouth Council for New England, David Thomson had plenty of opportunity to hear about the lands across the Atlantic. In 1622, he applied for a land grant. The council awarded him the grant on the condition that he remain on the land for five years.

Thomson and his wife, along with eight other colonists, eagerly set sail for New Hampshire to establish the colony's first English settlement. They settled near the mouth of the Piscataqua River, at a spot they called

European Exploration of New Hampshire

The colored arrows on this map show the routes taken by explorers between 1605 and 1614.

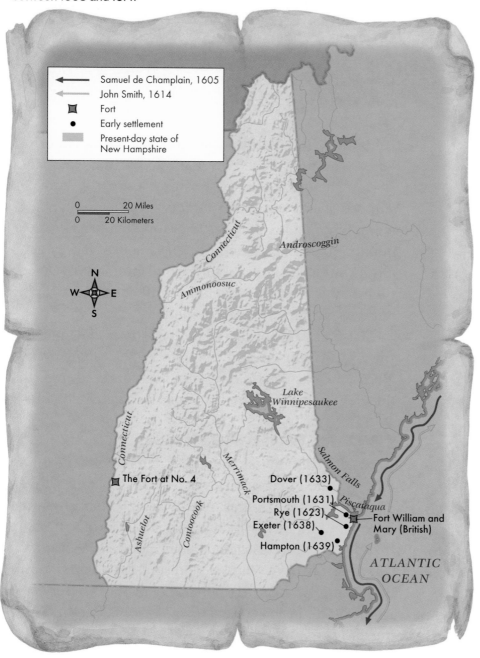

Samuel de Champlain, 1605
John Smith, 1614
Fort
Early settlement
Present-day state of New Hampshire

0   20 Miles
0   20 Kilometers

N
W   E
S

Androscoggin

Connecticut

Ammonoosuc

Lake Winnipesaukee

Connecticut

Merrimack

The Fort at No. 4

Salmon Falls

Dover (1633)

Portsmouth (1631)
Rye (1623)
Exeter (1638)

Piscataqua

Fort William and Mary (British)

Hampton (1639)

Ashuelot

Contoocook

ATLANTIC OCEAN

Portsmouth Harbor in 1640

Pannaway. Today, the location is known as Odiorne's Point. The men fished for giant cod in the waters offshore. They dried the fish on racks in the sun and shipped it in barrels to markets back in England. As winter approached, the settlers constructed a two-story building that they called the great house. It was actually a simple log house with a stone foundation. During their first winter in New Hampshire, it served as living quarters for the entire settlement.

Business did not go well for the settlers at Pannaway. In 1624, Thomson and his wife moved south to the Massachusetts Bay Colony. Other settlers scattered, and the great house and the fish racks stood abandoned.

TWO NEW HAMPSHIRES

In 1623, a London fish merchant named Edward Hilton founded the village of Dover on the Piscataqua River. Six years later, Gorges and Mason established the Laconia Company, which sent a shipload of settlers to the mouth of the Piscataqua near the site of Pannaway. There Strawbery Banke (present-day Portsmouth) began as a fishing settlement. The town of Exeter arose in 1638. Life in the coastal towns revolved around fishing and shipbuilding.

Further inland, farmers began to settle in the Merrimack Valley. The Connecticut Valley in the west was the remote frontier, but even there farms began to appear.

Each of the New Hampshire settlements operated on its own, with no centralized government. In 1641, the various towns agreed to come under the control of the Massachusetts colony. New Hampshire did not become a separate colony until 1691. When that happened, the British Crown appointed New Hampshire Colony's president and governing council, but the people of the colony elected members to a lower governing body called the Assembly.

Meanwhile, settlement progressed slowly in New Hampshire. Part of the problem was that John Mason's heirs continued to wrangle over land titles and boundaries. Few people wanted to risk applying for land grants that might later be swept away in a legal settlement. While Massachusetts grew and prospered, New Hampshire remained a scattering of quiet villages and farms.

In 1647, New Hampshire passed a law requiring that every town of 50 families or more must open a school. The law explained that education was necessary since "the chief project of Satan [is] to keep men from the knowledge of the Scripture" and so that "learning may not be buried in the grave of our fathers." The first schools were housed in barns or one-room cabins, and classes were usually taught by young men. Later, more and more women became teachers, usually hired at about half the salary that men were paid for the same work.

Early New Hampshire schools might have looked something like this.

THE WITCH OF HAMPTON

During the early years of colonial New England, belief in witchcraft was widespread. Between 1647 and 1692, 36 supposed witches were executed in Massachusetts and Connecticut, and hundreds were put on trial. Only one person was ever convicted of witchcraft in colonial New Hampshire. In 1656, Eunice Cole (1590?–1680?) of Hampton was tried for witchcraft and found guilty. She was sent to prison for 15 years. Her husband died while she was in prison, and after she was released, she lived her final years in poverty. Legends about Cole's hauntings and mischief persisted for generations.

The first enslaved Africans had reached New Hampshire in 1645. Most enslaved people worked for white families in their fields, homes, and businesses. To ensure they would not run away, laws were passed that forbade slaves to travel or stay out past a certain hour. Enslaved people were not allowed to hold public gatherings because they might make plans to flee or revolt. Some, like Amos Fortune and his wife, were able to buy their freedom by working extra hours for pay.

WEALTH FROM THE LAND

Just as John Smith had predicted, New Hampshire had riches in fish, furs, and timber. By the 1640s, the Isles of Shoals were a thriving center for drying, salting, and packing cod for export. Fur traders from Europe worked with Indians to trap beavers, martens, foxes, and other animals whose pelts were prized in Europe. Indians traded furs for guns, pots, and other European goods.

New Hampshire's greatest wealth lay in its pine forests. In some places, giant pines towered 150 to 200 feet (46 by 61 m) high, their massive trunks up to 6 feet (1.8 m) across. The trunks of these spectacular trees made perfect masts for sailing ships. The British navy constantly needed mast logs. As more and more of the tall trees were chopped down, the remaining trees became immensely valuable. A British law passed in 1729 reserved the best trees for the navy. A surveyor marked these special trees with three hatchet strokes,

cutting a broad arrow into the bark. The colonists resented this law and sometimes ignored it, cutting marked trees for their own use.

CLASHING CULTURES

At first, the English settlers were welcomed by New Hampshire's Indians. Pennacook leader Passaconaway and other Abenakis hoped that the English would be their friends and serve as allies against their enemies the Mohawk people, who lived to the west. Native people were eager to acquire guns and other trade goods from the newcomers. The English, in turn, wanted beaver pelts, which sold for high prices on European markets. For more than 50 years, English and

Logging became a big business in the mountains of New Hampshire.

WOW

Pine logs used for masts were sometimes 150 feet (46 m) long and enormously heavy and hard to move. A team of 90 or 100 oxen was needed to pull a single pine log out of the forest!

MINI-BIO

PASSACONAWAY: LEADER IN WAR AND PEACE

Little is known of the early life of Passaconaway (1570?–1679?), who became chief of the Pennacook people in about 1620. He led his people in a series of successful battles against the Mohawk people. But as English settlers poured into New England, he realized that warfare against them was hopeless. He worked to promote peace between Pennacooks and English colonists. Native Americans regarded Passaconaway as a great magician. According to legend, he could make water burn and cause trees to dance. In 1662, the Massachusetts legislature sold Passaconaway a piece of land on the Merrimack River, where he lived out his final years. Some legends say he lived to be more than 100 years old.

❓ Want to know more? See www.seacoastnh.com/History/As_I_Please/Tracking_Passaconaway/

Indians traded peacefully. English settlements were chiefly along the coast, and there was plenty of land for everyone.

As more English settlers arrived, they plowed up Native American hunting grounds and frightened away the game. English pigs and cattle sometimes plundered Indian cornfields.

In 1675, Metacom, a Wampanoag chief from Massachusetts, led an uprising against the colonists called King Philip's War. (The English referred to Metacom as King Philip.) Fighting spread through New England. The Pennacook people in New Hampshire stayed out of the war, but other groups led attacks against Durham, Exeter, and Hampton. A bitter winter finally slowed the fighting. When Metacom was killed in August 1676, the war ended.

English authorities decided to eliminate any future Indian threat. The government in Boston ordered Major Richard Waldron to seize as many Indians as he could. According to one story, Waldron invited about 400 Pennacooks to a series of athletic contests at the fort in Cochecho. When the unsuspecting Indians entered the fort, the English attacked. Several Indians were killed, and many others were captured and forced into slavery.

Among the survivors of the incident was Wonalancet, a son of Passaconaway. Passaconaway had counseled

After capturing and murdering numerous Pennacooks, Major Richard Waldron was killed in a surprise attack.

peace, but now Wonalancet hungered for revenge. In 1689, Pennacook fighters launched a surprise attack on Cochecho. Major Waldron was captured and killed. At the same time, Pennacooks spared a white woman named Elizabeth Heard who had earlier rescued an Indian and hidden him in her home. Her kindness was remembered and rewarded.

WAR AND SETTLEMENT

During the 1700s, Great Britain fought a series of wars with France. This conflict spilled into North America, where French and English colonists fought over timber, fishing grounds, and the fur trade. The French, who had settlements in eastern Canada, encouraged Abenakis to attack English farms and villages along the Connecticut and Merrimack rivers. Native Americans made lightning raids on isolated cabins and villages.

ROBERT ROGERS: "THE WHITE DEVIL"

When he was eight years old, Robert Rogers (1731–1795) moved with his family from Massachusetts to today's Dunbarton, New Hampshire. Fighting between colonists and Native Americans was frequent, and Rogers grew up amid war. In 1754, he organized a group of frontier fighters called Rogers' Rangers. Fighting in the woods, often traveling on snowshoes, the Rangers were highly effective soldiers, and Native Americans nicknamed Rogers the White Devil. Rogers led a series of attacks on French Canada and destroyed the fort at St. Francis in 1759. After the American Revolution, he settled in London, where he died in poverty.

? **Want to know more?** See www.rogersrangers.org/rogers/

WORD TO KNOW

guerrilla *a soldier who doesn't belong to a regular army; guerrillas often use surprise attacks and other uncommon battle tactics*

English colonists in New Hampshire fought back. In 1754, Robert Rogers organized a team of **guerrilla** fighters called Rogers' Rangers. The Rangers pushed their way into Canada and captured the key French and Indian settlement at St. Francis.

From 1754 to 1763, the conflict between the British and the French for control of North America became what is known as the French and Indian War. After the British won the war, most Native Americans in New Hampshire moved north into Canada. This was a turning point for New Hampshire. Settlers swarmed into the interior and rapidly laid out new towns. Within a little more than a dozen years, however, a war to win independence was at their doorstep.

GROWING UNREST

The years of fighting with France left the British treasury depleted. Parliament, the legislature in Great Britain, was eager to find new ways to raise money. One solution was to tax people living in the British colonies that stretched along the Atlantic coast from New Hampshire to Georgia.

In 1765, Great Britain passed a law called the Stamp Act. This law required colonists to purchase an official government stamp for documents such as wills and deeds. The colonists were outraged. They had no representatives in Parliament, and they believed that Parliament had no right to tax them when they could not elect anyone to represent their interests.

In Portsmouth, angry colonists burned an **effigy** of the stamp tax agent. They seized the stamps and locked them away where they could not be used. After similar protests throughout the colonies, Great Britain **repealed** the Stamp Act in 1766.

Parliament was still determined to tax the colonies, however, and issued the Townshend Acts. These were a series of laws taxing various imported items, including tea, glass, paint, and molasses. Once again, the colonists rose up in angry protest.

On October 29, 1771, a band of protesters boarded a British ship in Portsmouth Harbor. The ship carried a cargo of molasses, which could not be brought ashore

CHANGING BOUNDARIES

In 1764, the British king declared that the land west of the Connecticut River belonged not to New Hampshire, but to New York. The people of the region felt more connected to New Hampshire and were dismayed by the king's ruling. Eventually, in 1791, the area in question became the state of Vermont.

WORDS TO KNOW

effigy *a figure of a person or animal*

repealed *withdrew, undid*

New Hampshire

5

Stamp Master in Effigy

Angry residents of New Hampshire hang an effigy of the stamp agent during a protest in 1765.

until the taxes were paid. The protestors had disguised themselves by painting their faces. They seized the barrels of molasses and hauled them ashore. The British never caught the protesters and never collected any taxes on the molasses.

In 1773, angry colonists in nearby Boston dumped chests of tea overboard rather than pay the British import tax. As punishment for this incident, called the Boston Tea Party, Great Britain sent warships to blockade Boston Harbor. No colonial ships could move in or out. The British also sent troops to keep the rebels in Massachusetts under control.

NEW HAMPSHIRE AT WAR

On December 12, 1774, rebels in Boston learned of British plans to send troops to strengthen Fort William and Mary at the harbor in Portsmouth. A Boston silversmith named Paul Revere set out for Portsmouth on horseback. Revere galloped into Portsmouth and raised the alarm that British **redcoats** were on their way.

WORD TO KNOW

redcoats *British soldiers, especially during the American Revolution*

PAUL REVERE'S RIDES

On April 18, 1775, Paul Revere rode from Boston to the Massachusetts towns of Lexington and Concord to warn the people that the British were coming. Henry Wadsworth Longfellow made this historic ride famous in a poem. Yet Revere's first ride of warning occurred four months earlier, when he galloped from Boston to Portsmouth.

Paul Revere on horseback

About 400 New Hampshire colonists armed with clubs and muskets surged toward the fort, which was manned by only five British soldiers. When the British troops arrived a few days later, they found that the colonists had stripped the fort of its guns and other military supplies.

John Wentworth, royal governor of New Hampshire Colony

On April 19, 1775, gunfire erupted between a group of colonists and British troops in Lexington, Massachusetts. The American Revolution had begun. Each of the 13 American colonies recruited troops for the Continental army. New Hampshire farmers and fishermen, European Americans, and African Americans rushed to join. One soldier recalled, "We all set out with what weapons we could get, going like a flock of wild geese, we hardly knew why or whither."

Royal governor John Wentworth loved New Hampshire, where he had been born and raised, and had spent many years improving life for its people. At the same time, however, he was deeply loyal to the king. As the unrest mounted, Wentworth tried to bring the rebelling colonists under control. Ignoring his authority, the colonists formed their own legislature at Exeter. The rebel government sent delegates to the Continental Congress in Philadelphia.

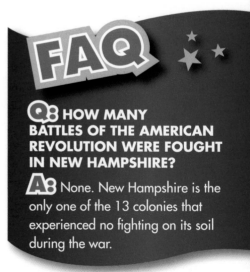

FAQ

Q8 HOW MANY BATTLES OF THE AMERICAN REVOLUTION WERE FOUGHT IN NEW HAMPSHIRE?

A8 None. New Hampshire is the only one of the 13 colonies that experienced no fighting on its soil during the war.

MINI-BIO

JOHN STARK: HERO OF THE REVOLUTION

In 1752, John Stark (1728–1822) was captured by Abenakis while hunting on the Pemigewasset River. The Abenakis were so impressed by Stark's bravery that they adopted him into their nation. Stark later fought with Rogers' Rangers during the French and Indian War. He commanded the First New Hampshire Regiment in the American Revolution, and in 1777 he became brigadier general of the New Hampshire **militia**. As he marched his troops into the Battle of Bennington in present-day Vermont, he exclaimed, "There are your enemies, the redcoats and the **Tories**. They are ours, or this night Molly Stark sleeps a widow!" Stark's men defeated the enemy at Bennington and helped weaken the British in the north. Stark is New Hampshire's greatest hero of the American Revolution.

 Want to know more? See www.nh.gov/nhdhr/publications/warheroes/starkj.html

WORDS TO KNOW

militia *an army made up of citizens trained to serve as soldiers in an emergency*

Tories *people who remained loyal to the British during the American Revolution*

privateers *private citizens given government approval to capture enemy ships*

By June 1775, Wentworth realized that his position was hopeless. He no longer had any authority in the colony he had tried so hard to serve. He left New Hampshire forever, eventually settling in Nova Scotia, Canada.

With Governor Wentworth's resignation, New Hampshire was on its own. In January 1776, it became the first of the 13 colonies to adopt a state constitution. On June 15 of the same year, the New Hampshire legislature voted to urge the Continental Congress to call for independence from Great Britain. And on July 4, New Hampshire delegates joined representatives from the other colonies in signing the Declaration of Independence.

During the Revolution, soldiers from New Hampshire served in every major battle. Portsmouth shipyards built three vessels for the Continental navy. Barges called gundalows, which could be rowed or sailed, were used for shipping supplies on inland and coastal waters. Some 3,000 New Hampshire sailors became **privateers** during the war. Sailing in armed vessels along the Atlantic coast, they attacked British supply ships, capturing their cargoes for the rebels.

THE NINTH STATE

In 1783, Great Britain and the former colonies signed a peace treaty. The 13 colonies were now an independent nation, the United States of America. For the next four years, the United States struggled to form an effective government.

Meanwhile, New Hampshire had government problems of its own. The people of the Connecticut Valley believed that the 1776 constitution did not give them enough voice in state government. The year after the constitution was adopted, the 36 towns in this region **seceded** from New Hampshire and formed their own **republic**. The towns rejoined New Hampshire in 1782,

Portsmouth shipyards were busy producing vessels during the American Revolution.

WORDS TO KNOW

seceded *withdrew from a group or an organization*

republic *a nation in which citizens can vote; republics are usually led by presidents*

George Washington (center) presiding over the Constitutional Convention of 1787

Wentworth Cheswell, an African American veteran of the Revolutionary War, was among the leading citizens of the town of Newmarket. He was elected to the town school board, as a **selectman**, and to other offices in the 1770s and 1780s.

WORD TO KNOW

selectman *an official elected to help run a New England town*

but their rebellion awakened the state legislature to the need for reform. In 1784, New Hampshire adopted a new constitution, which gave the western towns more representation. Though amended, or changed, slightly since then, that constitution—with its wariness of strong central government—is still in effect in New Hampshire today.

In the summer of 1787, delegates from the 13 states met in Philadelphia, Pennsylvania, to hammer out a national constitution. To be accepted, the constitution required the approval of two-thirds of the states. On June 21, 1788, New Hampshire became the ninth state to ratify the Constitution. This made the U.S. Constitution the law of the land.

New Hampshire: From Colony to State
(1763–1788)

This map shows the 13 original colonies and the area outlined in green that became the state of New Hampshire in 1788.

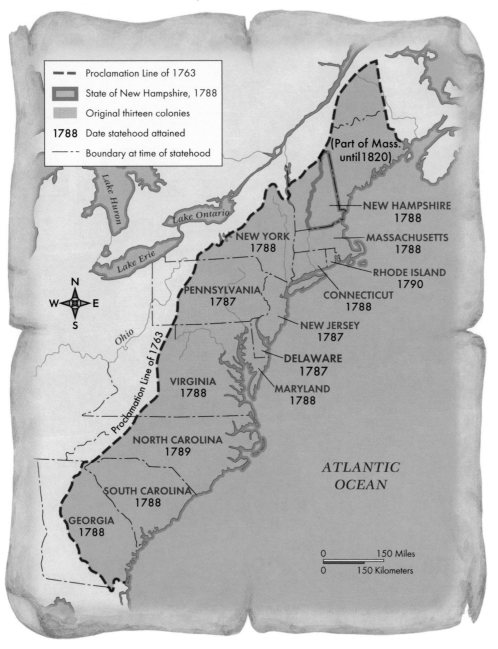

Proclamation Line of 1763
State of New Hampshire, 1788
Original thirteen colonies
1788 Date statehood attained
Boundary at time of statehood

Lake Huron

Lake Ontario

Lake Erie

(Part of Mass. until 1820)

NEW HAMPSHIRE 1788

MASSACHUSETTS 1788

RHODE ISLAND 1790

NEW YORK 1788

CONNECTICUT 1788

PENNSYLVANIA 1787

NEW JERSEY 1787

Ohio

DELAWARE 1787

VIRGINIA 1788

MARYLAND 1788

Proclamation Line of 1763

NORTH CAROLINA 1789

ATLANTIC OCEAN

SOUTH CAROLINA 1788

GEORGIA 1788

N W E S

0   150 Miles
0   150 Kilometers

READ ABOUT

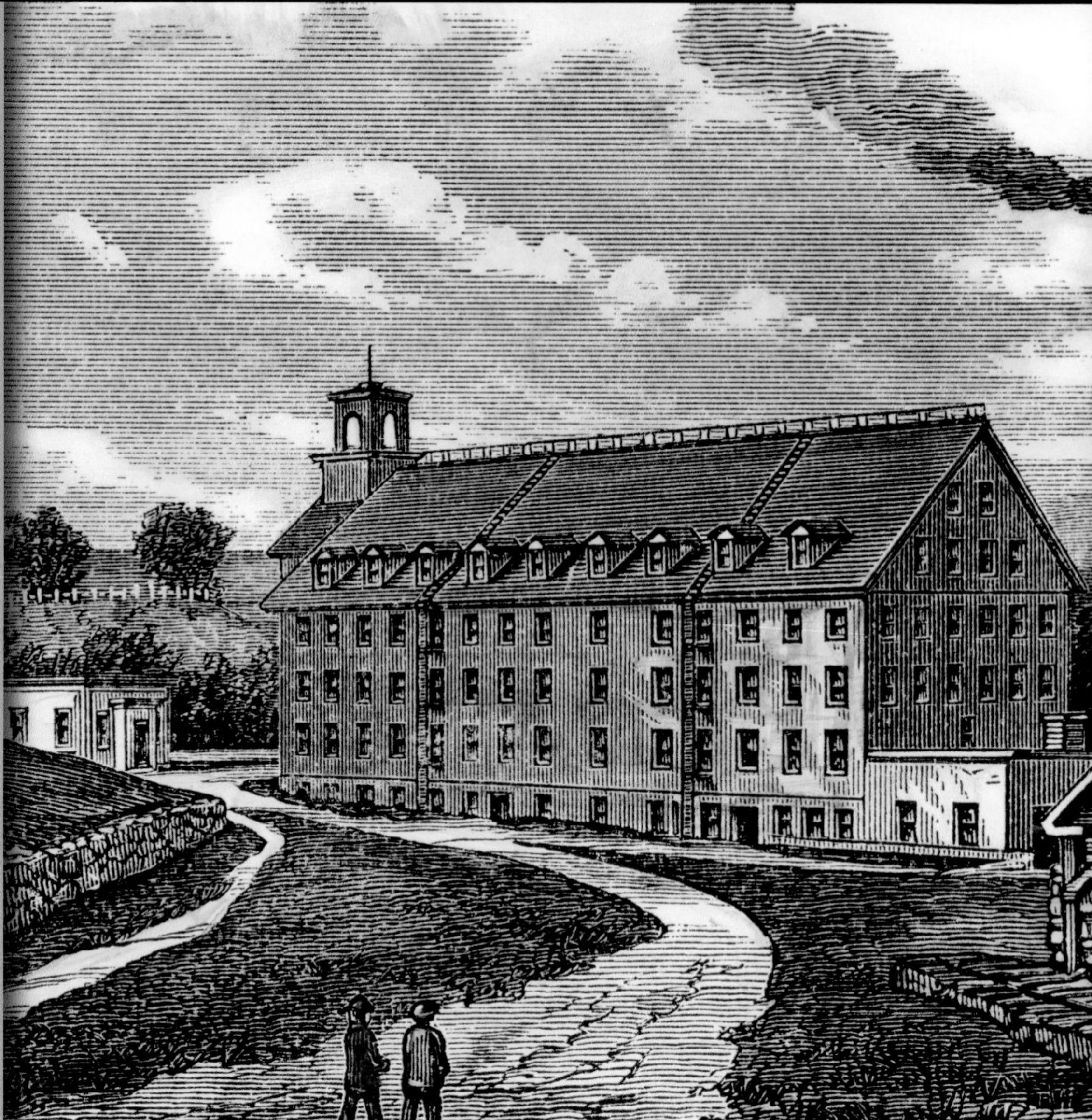

Sugar River textile mills in Newport

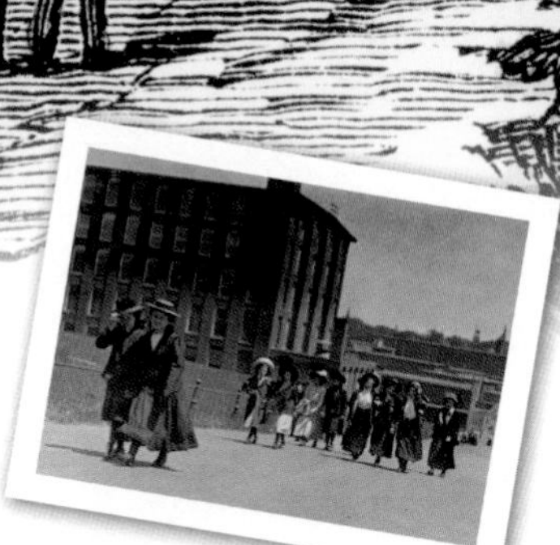

1808

Concord becomes New Hampshire's capital

1820s ▲

Textile mills open in many New Hampshire towns, employing thousands of girls and young women

1832

Settlers in northern New Hampshire establish the Republic of Indian Stream

CHAPTER FOUR

GROWTH AND CHANGE

★

AT THE BEGINNING OF THE 19TH CENTURY, THE RESIDENTS OF NEW HAMPSHIRE WORKED HARD. Farmers hoed and plowed, sowed and harvested, much as their grandparents had done before. Yet New Hampshire stood on the brink of change. Factories and railroads would soon carry the state into the age of industry.

1852 ▶

Franklin Pierce of Hillsborough is elected the 14th U.S. president

1880s

The Boston and Maine Railroad gains control of the New Hampshire railroad industry

1890s

The Amoskeag Manufacturing Company is the world's biggest producer of cotton cloth

A small farm in Franconia Notch, mid-1800s

TILLING THE SOIL

Although New Hampshire has rocky soil and a rather short growing season, more and more of its land was plowed under and turned into farmland in the early decades of the 19th century. Farmers in southern New Hampshire raised a variety of crops including corn, beans, wheat, barley, and hay.

As farming grew in importance, New Hampshirites decided to move the state capital from Portsmouth to the town of Concord in the Merrimack Valley. In 1819, the legislature met for the first time at Concord in the newly built State House.

As the United States expanded westward, New Hampshire farmers heard tales of rich land on the prairies of Indiana, Illinois, and Iowa. In the 1830s, hundreds of New Hampshire families packed up and joined the great migration west.

MILLS ON THE RIVER

In colonial days, New Hampshire women worked long hours spinning flax into linen thread, which was woven into cloth. They also spun the wool of sheep into thread. In the early 1800s, spinning wheels disappeared as machines in textile mills produced thread and cloth. Mills opened in Dover, Exeter, Nashua, and Somersworth in the 1820s. In the 1830s, a group of Boston investors set up a textile factory at Amoskeag Falls on the Merrimack River. The falls generated power to operate a variety of spinning and weaving machines.

Companies recruited young women from nearby villages to work in the mills. Most girls had usually stayed at home until they married and started families. Now, a generation of teens and young women had the chance to move away from their parents and earn money on their own. Many of them found the freedom thrilling. But the work was hard, and the pay was low. Mill girls usually worked at their machines 13 hours a day, six days a week.

In 1828, a group of women went on **strike** at a cotton mill in Dover. They were the first women to organize a strike in U.S. history.

WORD TO KNOW

strike *an organized refusal to work, usually as a sign of protest about working conditions*

TRADE UNIONIST

Sarah Bagley (1806–1883), who grew up in Candia, New Hampshire, was the first woman in the United States to establish a trade union, a workers' organization that bargained for better wages and labor conditions. Bagley went to work in the textile mills of Lowell, Massachusetts, in 1836. In 1844, she founded the 600-member Lowell Female Labor Reform Association to demand improvements such as reducing the workday to 10 hours. Bagley left her factory job, but she did not fall silent. She traveled throughout Massachusetts and New Hampshire, encouraging millworkers to speak out and establishing branches of the Female Labor Reform Association. Because of her efforts, some factory owners eventually shortened the workday to 11 hours, but not to 10. In 1846, Bagley became the nation's first woman telegraph operator.

Women and girls on their way to work at Amoskeag Manufacturing Company

WORDS TO KNOW

famines *periods of extreme food shortages and hunger*

underground railroad *a secret network of people who helped those fleeing slavery reach freedom*

THE REPUBLIC OF INDIAN STREAM

After the American Revolution, both the United States and Canada claimed the land at New Hampshire's northern tip. For 60 years, disputes flared over the territory but were not resolved. At last, in 1832, the settlers in the region declared their independence. They established their own nation, the Republic of Indian Stream, with its own legislature and courthouse. Three years later, New Hampshire sent 20 militia members to invade the republic. The Indian Stream leaders surrendered without bloodshed, and the republic became part of New Hampshire. A treaty officially settled the boundary dispute with Canada in 1842.

During the 1840s, terrible **famines** in Ireland led to massive starvation. Desperate to build a better life, thousands of people left Ireland and settled in the United States. Many young Irish women found work in the mills of Manchester and other New Hampshire towns. Later, newcomers from Poland, Greece, Italy, and other European countries joined them. French-speaking immigrants from Quebec in Canada also moved to New Hampshire in search of jobs. Many of them, especially women, found work in the textile factories.

THE NATION DIVIDED

In the 1830s and 1840s, tension mounted in the United States over the issue of slavery. Though the enslavement of African Americans had largely ended in Northern states, it remained deeply rooted in the South. As a movement to abolish, or end, slavery gathered strength in the North, the Southern slaveholders raised a fierce resistance. In New Hampshire, many towns had anti-slavery societies and **underground railroad** stations to help those who escaped slavery find liberty.

As the United States grew, arguments raged in Congress over whether slavery should be allowed in the western territories. Some feared the conflict would break the Union apart. In 1850, New Hampshire native Daniel Webster offered a compromise. Under the Compromise of 1850, California entered the Union as a Free State (one that banned slavery), but the new law also included the Fugitive Slave Act to please Southern slaveholders. This act made it a crime to help an escaped slave. Many people in the North strenuously objected to being forced to capture people seeking freedom.

Another New Hampshirite who tried to resolve the growing differences between North and South was

MINI-BIO

DANIEL WEBSTER: LEGENDARY ORATOR

Daniel Webster (1782–1852) was born in Salisbury, today part of Franklin. He graduated from Dartmouth College and became a lawyer. He later was elected to the U.S. House of Representatives and to the U.S. Senate. In Washington, Webster worked tirelessly to keep the Union together. He crafted the Compromise of 1850 in an attempt to please both the North and the South. He was one of the most eloquent speakers ever to set foot in Congress, and his speeches are still read and admired today.

? Want to know more? See www.dartmouth. edu/~dwebster/

The Third New Hampshire Infantry at a military camp in South Carolina, 1862

Franklin Pierce, a lawyer and politician. Pierce believed that slavery was wrong, but he thought that states had the right to choose whether they would allow slavery or not. In 1852, Pierce was elected president of the United States as a compromise candidate who appealed to voters on both sides of the slavery issue.

All the efforts of leaders such as Webster and Pierce failed to prevent war. In December 1860, South Carolina seceded from the Union. Ten other Southern states soon followed, and they formed a new nation, the Confederate States of America. The bloody Civil War began in April 1861, when Confederate soldiers fired

FAQ

Q8 HOW LONG DID SLAVERY CONTINUE IN NEW HAMPSHIRE?

A8 In 1790, there were 157 enslaved African Americans living in New Hampshire. That number dwindled over the years, and slavery was outlawed in the state in 1857.

MINI-BIO

HARRIET DAME: NURSE TO THE WOUNDED

At the outbreak of the Civil War, Harriet Dame (1815–1900) of Barnstead was a seamstress who ran a boardinghouse. When she read a notice asking women to volunteer as army nurses, she answered the call. Dame had no training as a nurse, but she learned through experience. During most of the war, she cared for the sick and wounded of the Second New Hampshire Regiment. Her skills were so impressive that she was sent to inspect and recommend improvements for army hospitals in Washington and South Carolina. One of her patients described her as "the bravest, sweetest, and best-beloved" nurse in the Union. In 1901, the New Hampshire legislature commissioned a portrait of Harriet Dame. It was the first portrait of a woman to hang in the State House.

 Want to know more? See www.nh.gov/nhdhr/publications/warheroes/dameh.html

WOW

In the 1890s, workers at the Amoskeag Manufacturing Company turned out 1 mile (1.6 km) of cotton fabric per minute!

on Union-held Fort Sumter in Charleston, South Carolina.

No Civil War battles were fought in New Hampshire, but some 35,000 New Hampshirites, both African American and European American, joined the military to fight for the Union. Historians estimate that half the men in New Hampshire served in the military during the war years. With so many men away, more responsibility than ever fell on the shoulders of New Hampshire women. Besides cooking, sewing, and caring for children, they worked the fields and ran family businesses.

THE PACE QUICKENS

In the years after the Civil War, the textile industry grew in Manchester and other New Hampshire towns. New machines helped workers become faster and more productive than ever. By the 1890s, the Amoskeag Manufacturing Company was the biggest producer of cotton cloth in the world.

In northern New Hampshire, logging companies began to harvest the dense, untouched forests. By now, the great pines used for masts had all disappeared. The spruce and fir trees that grew in the northern woods did not yield strong timber for building houses, but

Inside the card room of Amoskeag Manufacturing Company, where cotton cloth was produced, late 1800s

their relatively soft wood was perfect for the manufacture of paper. Logging companies cleared great swaths of forest. They shipped the fresh logs to paper mills on the Androscoggin and other New England rivers, leaving fields of stumps behind them.

Farmers, loggers, and manufacturers needed to ship their goods to market. Railways were the most efficient method of transportation. In 1874, New Hampshire had 893 miles (1,437 km) of railroad tracks. Trains went almost everywhere, but getting from one place to another could be very complicated because the tracks belonged to 32 different companies. In the 1880s, one powerful railroad company, the Boston and Maine, bought up the other lines and took control of freight and passenger service in New Hampshire.

Trains transported people, as well as lumber and manufactured goods, as New Hampshire grew.

Officials of the Boston and Maine found clever ways to make New Hampshire serve railroad owners. They bribed politicians with free train passes and hired the state's most talented lawyers. The state legislature allowed the company to pay low taxes and charge high fares. In the 1880s, William E. Chandler, owner of the *New Hampshire Statesman* and the *Concord Evening Monitor*, raised his voice in concern about the company's growing power. In one editorial, he wrote, "[The railroads] will rule New Hampshire with a rod of iron. They will control both political parties, destroy every newspaper, [hire] every lawyer, nominate every legislator and fill his pockets with free passes."

In 1887, Chandler was elected to represent New Hampshire in the U.S. Senate. In Washington, he continued to battle railroad **monopolies** in New Hampshire and throughout the nation. Eventually, state and federal laws forbade bribery and broke monopolies into smaller, less powerful companies.

WORD TO KNOW

monopolies *companies that control the entire supply of a particular good or service*

GETTING AWAY FROM IT ALL

Though factories and railroads quickened New Hampshire's pace of life, the state was still a haven of sparkling lakes, clear air, and stunning mountain scenery. In the 1880s and 1890s, people from Boston and New York discovered the delights of vacationing in New Hampshire. Some rented rooms from farm families. Others enjoyed gracious living at elegant hotels on Lake Winnipesaukee and in the White Mountains.

A few wealthy families built summer homes on New Hampshire's lakes. These were no mere cottages, but magnificent mansions with high ceilings and massive stone fireplaces. When they took the train to New Hampshire in the summer, these families brought dozens of trunks filled with clothes, books, toys, and china. They also brought their servants—cooks, housemaids, and nursemaids to care for the children. In the woods of New Hampshire, they lived with all the luxuries of home.

By the end of the 19th century, many people realized that New Hampshire was a great vacation spot.

READ ABOUT

Workers fill orders
at B. W. Kilburn
and Company
in Littleton

1911

New Hampshire passes
a strong law limiting
child labor

▲**1911**

The federal government
establishes White
Mountain National
Forest in northern New
Hampshire

1922

Workers at
the Amoskeag
Manufacturing
Company go on
strike

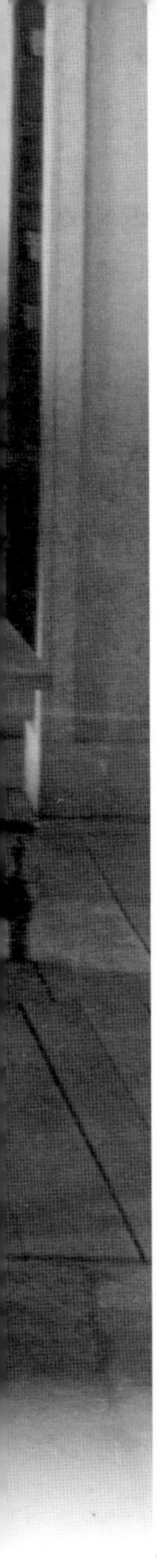

CHAPTER FIVE

MORE MODERN TIMES

★

A S THE 20TH CENTURY BEGAN, CHANGES WERE IN STORE FOR NEW HAMPSHIRE. No longer reliant only on mills, New Hampshirites of every background had different paths to follow. During World War II, many women took jobs in industry, and cities blossomed as people left the countryside to find new jobs and new opportunities.

1941–1945

The Portsmouth Naval Shipyard builds hundreds of vessels during World War II

1990 ▲

A nuclear power plant opens at Seabrook after a 17-year battle with environmentalists

2008

Nearly 530,000 people vote in the New Hampshire presidential primary

Photographer Lewis Hine captured images of young workers, such as this 12-year-old cotton spinner.

WORD TO KNOW

canneries *factories where food is canned*

UP FROM THE ASHES

In 1903, a series of forest fires raged across northern New Hampshire and western Maine. Uncontrolled logging had set the stage for such fires by leaving large open areas studded with dry stumps and fallen branches. The 1903 fires helped the public see the need to protect New England's forests. In 1911, the federal government established White Mountain National Forest in Maine and New Hampshire.

PROGRESS AND REFORM

In the early decades of the 20th century, thousands of people from southern and eastern Europe poured into the United States. Greeks, Italians, Poles, and others settled in Manchester and elsewhere in New Hampshire. Most took jobs in the state's textile mills. **Canneries** also employed newcomers to the nation.

In 1909 and 1911, a photographer named Lewis Hine visited New Hampshire. In a series of heart-wrenching photos, he captured the experience of children who worked in the state's mills and canneries. Hine's pictures awakened the public to the plight of child workers, some of them only eight or nine years old. In 1911, New Hampshire's governor, Robert P. Bass, signed a strong law limiting child labor. Other labor laws shortened the workday and improved safety on the job.

During the early 20th century, railroads began to face competition for transporting passengers and goods. With each passing year, more cars and trucks sped over a widening network of highways, taking more business away from the railroads. The arrival of the automobile diminished the power of the railroads in New Hampshire.

OVER THERE AND HOME AGAIN

In 1914, a devastating war erupted in Europe. For a time, the United States managed to stay out of the war, but in 1917 President Woodrow Wilson concluded that the United States had to help its European allies. Young men from all across the nation headed to Europe to fight. About 20,000 New Hampshirites joined the military and fought overseas. Many of them had never been more than a few miles from home.

During the war, the Portsmouth Naval Shipyard went into high gear. It turned out warships and a relatively new type of naval vessel, the submarine. The Portsmouth Naval Shipyard became a major center for submarine construction and repair.

World War I ended in November 1918. American soldiers returned home to a heroes' welcome, but they soon faced a sagging economy. The price of farm produce tumbled. Many factories cut workers' wages, resulting in a rash of strikes.

On February 2, 1922, workers at the Amoskeag Manufacturing Company received shocking news. Factory managers announced that wages would be cut by 20 percent. At the same time, employees would

SUFFRAGE FOR ALL

Under New Hampshire's first constitution, approved in 1776, both men and women enjoyed suffrage, or the right to vote. But New Hampshire women lost their voting rights in 1784. In 1902, male voters across New Hampshire defeated a law that would have given women the right to vote. Women in New Hampshire and across the country finally gained the right to vote in 1920, when the 19th Amendment to the U.S. Constitution became law.

be required to work an additional six hours per week. The combination of a pay cut and longer workweek enraged the millworkers. On February 13, 12,000 of the factory's 17,000 workers went on strike.

Through the nine long months of the strike, workers suffered and the company had to shut down the mill. The company lost millions of dollars. With no wages, workers faced hunger and other hardships. The company relented at last and offered the workers their former hours and wages. The strike was finally over.

DEPRESSION AND WAR

In 1929, the nation plunged into a severe economic depression. In New Hampshire and all across the country, farm prices fell, banks failed, and factories closed.

Governor John Winant supported New Deal programs and helped New Hampshire weather the Great Depression.

Workers from the Civilian Conservation Corps, a New Deal program, remove rocks from a road in the White Mountains, 1930s.

In 1936, the Amoskeag Manufacturing Company, which had never fully recovered from the strike, shut its doors forever.

To rescue the struggling nation, President Franklin D. Roosevelt created a series of federal programs called the New Deal. These programs hired hundreds of thousands of people to build roads, bridges, schools, libraries, and hospitals. New Hampshire's governor, John Winant, supported the New Deal and began many state-run programs to help the unemployed. He won the deep respect of most New Hampshirites.

On December 7, 1941, Japanese planes bombed the U.S. Navy fleet stationed at Pearl Harbor, Hawai'i. The attack pulled the nation into World War II. Frank Knox,

FROM BERLIN TO BERLIN

In 1944, 240 German prisoners of war were shipped to the tiny town of Stark, New Hampshire. Stark is 20 miles (32 km) from the paper-manufacturing town of Berlin, which bears the same name as the capital of Germany. For two years, the German prisoners worked as loggers in New Hampshire's northern forests.

"LIVE FREE OR DIE!"

Shortly before the end of World War I, New Hampshire's legislature adopted a state motto: "Live Free or Die!" The motto came from a toast offered in 1809 by General John Stark, New Hampshire's hero of the American Revolution. The full toast was, "Live free or die; death is not the worst of evils."

President Roosevelt's newly appointed secretary of the navy, was in charge of rebuilding the ravaged fleet. A native of Manchester, Knox turned to the Portsmouth Naval Shipyard for help. Portsmouth shipbuilders worked around the clock, constructing landing craft, floating cranes, and other vessels. At the height of the war, the shipyard managed to complete an astonishing two submarines a week!

Some 60,000 New Hampshirites of many backgrounds enlisted in the armed forces during the war. Back in New Hampshire, women did much of the work at the shipyards and defense plants.

The eyes of the world turned to New Hampshire in 1944, when representatives from 64 nations gathered in Bretton Woods to attend the International Monetary Conference. The attendees at the conference planned ways to regulate the world's money supply when the

The Mount Washington Hotel in Bretton Woods hosted the International Monetary Conference in 1944.

war was over. They agreed to establish the World Bank and the International Monetary Fund. To this day, these organizations provide financial and technical support to developing nations and help set rules for the international system of exchanging money.

CHANGES AND CHALLENGES

In 1945, World War II ended, and soldiers returned home to a swiftly changing world. More and more people were leaving farms to find work in urban areas. They took jobs in schools, hospitals, stores, and factories. As people flowed into urban areas, quiet New Hampshire villages blossomed into towns and small cities. Suburban communities spread out from Manchester and Concord. Some families even moved to New Hampshire from around Boston, Massachusetts. Although they enjoyed the scenery and more leisurely pace of the Granite State, they faced long commutes to and from work in Massachusetts.

In the late decades of the 20th century, New Hampshire struggled to balance the need for jobs and development against the need to protect its environment. In 1973, Greek businessman Aristotle Onassis tried to open a giant oil refinery at Durham Point, an expanse of forest on the Great Bay. Governor Meldrim Thomson strongly supported the project, promising that it would bring many much-needed jobs to the state. However, environmental activists believed that the refinery would cause irreparable damage to recreation areas and wildlife habitat. The people of Durham overwhelmingly voted the project down at a town meeting in 1974.

Environmentalists fought the opening of a nuclear power plant in the coastal town of Seabrook. Activists

MINI-BIO

CHRISTA McAULIFFE: TEACHER IN SPACE

From the time she was a girl, Christa McAuliffe (1948–1986) wanted to be an astronaut. But few women had ever blasted off into space, and McAuliffe suspected she would never have the opportunity. She became a high school teacher in Concord, but her fascination with space travel remained. When she learned that the National Aeronautics and Space Administration (NASA) wanted a teacher to fly on one of its missions, she rushed to apply. She was accepted into the space program and underwent rigorous training. On January 28, 1986, she and six other crew members were killed when the space shuttle Challenger exploded only moments after takeoff.

❓ **Want to know more?** See www.jsc.nasa.gov/Bios/htmlbios/mcauliffe.html

helped delay the project for 17 years, but in 1990 it finally went into operation. Since then, opposition has died down.

In 1949, New Hampshire's legislature passed a law requiring that the state's presidential primary election be held on the second Tuesday in March. As a result, New Hampshire became the first state to hold its primary elections in each presidential election year. In the years since, the state has moved its primaries earlier and earlier so it

Residents of Derry cast their votes in the 2008 Republican and Democratic primaries.

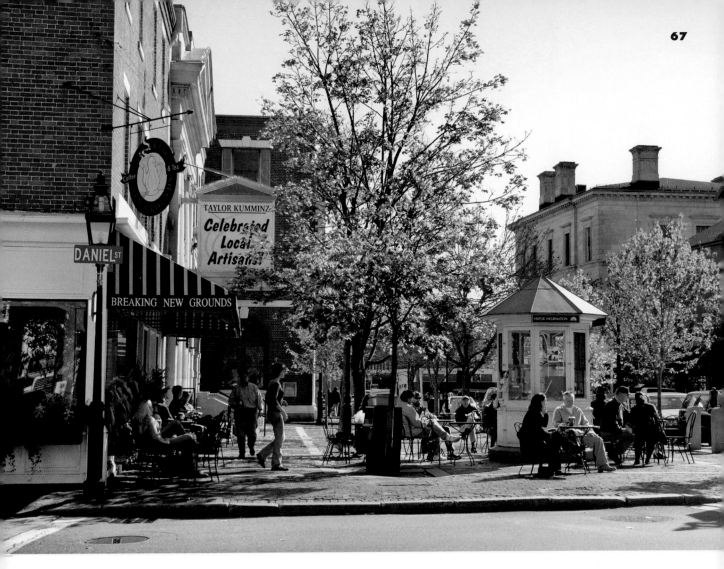

An outdoor café on Market Square in Portsmouth

can remain the first. The primary has become a major battleground for candidates. Those who do poorly often drop out of the race, while those who do well are thrust into the national spotlight.

In January 2008, almost 530,000 New Hampshirites went to the polls to vote in the Republican and Democratic presidential primaries. This was a record turnout, beating previous numbers by 25 percent. To this day, small though it is, New Hampshire plays a leading role in the selection of the nation's presidential candidates.

READ ABOUT

People gather
at the Pumpkin
Festival in Keene.

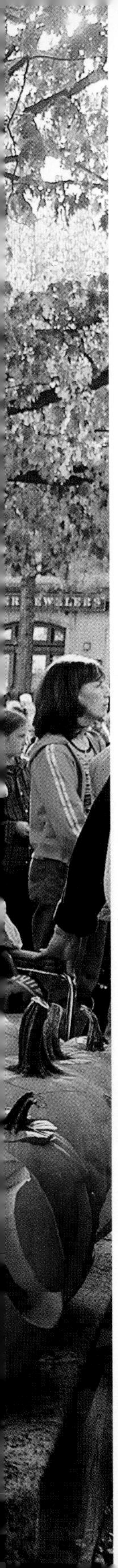

CHAPTER SIX

PEOPLE

★

IT HAS OFTEN BEEN SAID THAT NEW HAMPSHIRE'S NICKNAME, THE GRANITE STATE, REFERS TO THE CHARACTER OF ITS PEOPLE. New Hampshirites have a reputation for being as tough and stubborn as their state's stony hills. In reality, of course, people in New Hampshire are as varied as people anywhere else. Their unique backgrounds and talents have made the state what it is today.

LIVING IN NEW HAMPSHIRE

About 59 percent of all New Hampshirites are urban dwellers, meaning that they live in cities or towns of at least 2,500 people. New Hampshire's population is concentrated in two metropolitan areas. Nashua and its surrounding communities are an extension of the metropolitan area around Boston, Massachusetts. Manchester and the nearby towns are the second metropolitan area in the Granite State. In general, New Hampshire's population becomes less dense as you travel north. The state's northernmost counties have only a few towns scattered among deep forests.

People of French Canadian heritage live throughout the state. Other New Hampshirites have ancestors who

A family in Warner sits down for a meal.

THE YANKEE SPIRIT

People from New England, especially New Hampshire and Vermont, are sometimes referred to as Yankees. The history of the nickname is uncertain, but it may have originated from the Dutch name *Janke*, used to describe English and Dutch settlers in the New England states. During the Civil War, Southerners used the word, usually in a negative way, to refer to people from the Northern states. Since the American Revolution, the British have used the term in reference to all Americans. In some traditions, Yankees are said to be hardworking, stubborn, and unwilling to waste words.

A cooper, in the hardworking Yankee tradition, at the Strawbery Banke Museum in Portsmouth

came from Europe in the 19th and early 20th centuries. New Hampshirites are most likely to be of English, Irish, German, Italian, and Portuguese descent. Most Latinos in New Hampshire are of Mexican or Puerto Rican heritage. Many Asian Americans in the state have roots in China, Korea, India, and Pakistan.

People QuickFacts

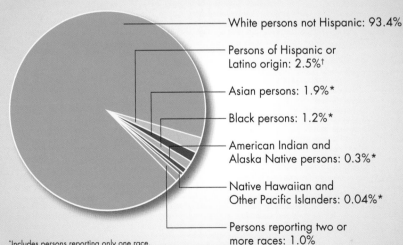

White persons not Hispanic: 93.4%

Persons of Hispanic or Latino origin: 2.5%†

Asian persons: 1.9%*

Black persons: 1.2%*

American Indian and Alaska Native persons: 0.3%*

Native Hawaiian and Other Pacific Islanders: 0.04%*

Persons reporting two or more races: 1.0%

*Includes persons reporting only one race.
†Hispanics may be of any race, so they are also included in applicable race categories.
Source: U.S. Census Bureau, 2007 estimate

Where New Hampshirites Live

The colors on this map indicate population density throughout the state. The darker the color, the more people live there.

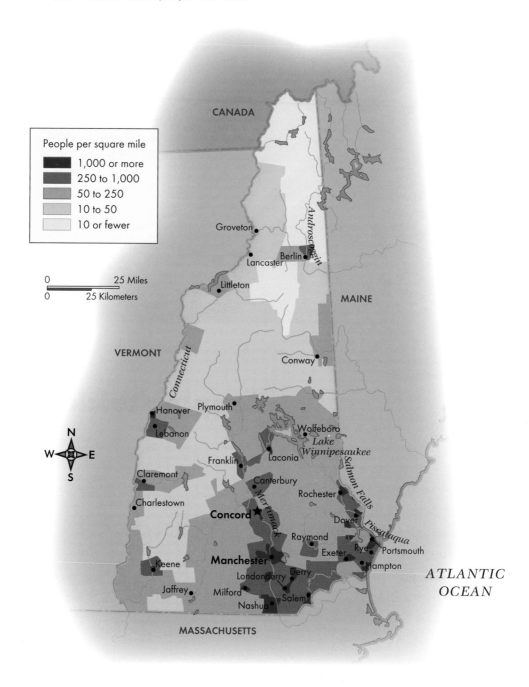

People per square mile

1,000 or more
250 to 1,000
50 to 250
10 to 50
10 or fewer

0   25 Miles
0   25 Kilometers

CANADA

Androscoggin

Groveton

Lancaster
Berlin

Littleton

MAINE

VERMONT

Connecticut

Conway

Hanover

Plymouth

Wolfeboro
Lake Winnipesaukee

Lebanon

Franklin

Laconia

Salmon Falls

Claremont

Canterbury

Rochester

Charlestown

Concord

Dover

Piscataqua

Merrimack

Raymond

Exeter
Rye
Portsmouth

Keene

Manchester

Londonderry
Derry

Hampton

ATLANTIC
OCEAN

Jaffrey

Milford

Salem

Nashua

MASSACHUSETTS

N
W   E
S

New Hampshire Population Growth

This chart shows New Hampshire's population changes between 1790 and 2000, and it projects that by 2010 there will be nearly 1.5 million people living in the state.

Source: U.S. Census Bureau

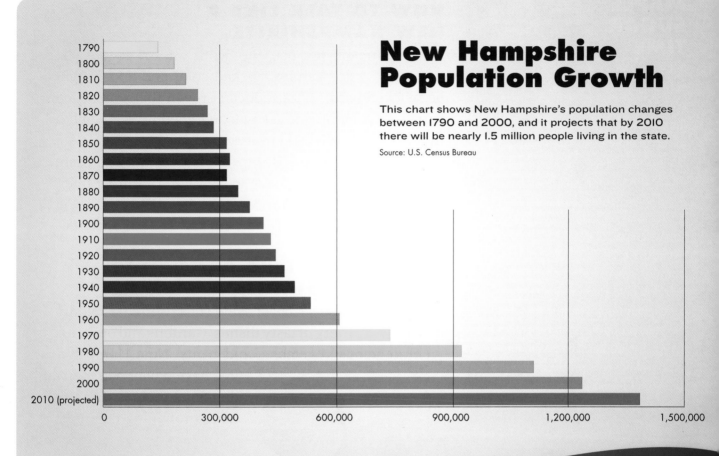

1790	
1800	
1810	
1820	
1830	
1840	
1850	
1860	
1870	
1880	
1890	
1900	
1910	
1920	
1930	
1940	
1950	
1960	
1970	
1980	
1990	
2000	
2010 (projected)	

0   300,000   600,000   900,000   1,200,000   1,500,000

Big City Life

This list shows the population of New Hampshire's biggest cities.

Manchester	109,691
Nashua	87,321
Concord	42,336
Rochester	30,004
Keene	22,778

Source: U.S. Census Bureau

Q: WHERE DID THE NAME NASHUA COME FROM?

A: The city of Nashua was named for the Nashua River. And the river got its name from the Nashuway Indians. The term comes from the Pennacook language and means "beautiful stream with a pebbly bottom."

Jars of maple syrup

MAPLE SUGAR TIME

Between late February and early April, the sap begins to run in New Hampshire's sugar maple trees. Long ago, Native Americans learned to make cuts on the trees and harvest the sweet sap as a special treat. Today, New Hampshirites enjoy "sugar on snow parties," where fresh boiled sap is drizzled onto clean snow to create a delicious treat. The first sap of the year produces light, delicate syrup. The darkest syrup with the strongest flavor is produced toward the end of the sugar season.

HOW TO TALK LIKE A NEW HAMPSHIRITE

New Hampshirites use the word *wicked* to suggest intensity. A day can be "wicked cold" and a job might be "wicked hard." *Wicked* doesn't mean that something is bad. A student can get "wicked good grades," and a movie can be "wicked fantastic!"

If you go to a New Hampshire restaurant and there are no seats, you may have to stand in a "waiting line." Your laundry room is probably in the "cellar," and you eat "supper" for your evening meal.

HOW TO EAT LIKE A NEW HAMPSHIRITE

With its lakes and seacoast, New Hampshire has plenty of fish for a variety of tasty dishes. Gardens and orchards yield delicious vegetables and fruits. New Hampshirites have developed many delicious recipes that use homegrown ingredients.

A worker harvests apples from a New Hampshire orchard.

MENU

WHAT'S ON THE MENU IN NEW HAMPSHIRE?

★ ★ ★

Creamy Pumpkin Soup

This favorite fall soup uses peeled, boiled pumpkin as a main ingredient. The pumpkin is blended with onion, celery, cream, and a dash of maple syrup.

Green Salad with Maple Syrup Dressing

A few tablespoons of maple syrup add a delightful flavor to dressing for a garden salad!

New England Clam Chowder

A blend of clams, potatoes, celery, and onion, thickened with flour and milk or cream. What could be better on a chilly evening?

New England clam chowder

TRY THIS RECIPE
Oven-Toasted Pumpkin Seeds

Pumpkin seeds are a tasty, healthy snack. Here's a quick and easy way to prepare them. Be sure to have an adult nearby to help.

Pumpkins

Ingredients:
1 pumpkin
Olive oil or melted butter
Salt, garlic powder, onion powder, or other seasoning of your choice

Instructions:
1. Have an adult cut open a pumpkin for you (it's very hard to slice through the rind).
2. Scoop out the pumpkin seeds and pulp.
3. In a colander, rinse and clean the pumpkin seeds, removing the pulp with your fingers. Dry on towels overnight.
4. Preheat the oven to 250°F.
5. Line a baking sheet with foil.
6. Toss the pumpkin seeds in olive oil or butter. Sprinkle with seasoning.
7. Bake about 1 hour, stirring every 15 minutes, until golden brown.
8. Eat them warm or store them in an airtight container. At room temperature, they will keep for three months. Stored in the refrigerator, they will keep for up to a year!

Students on the Dartmouth College campus in Hanover

Dartmouth College is the ninth-oldest college in the United States.

EDUCATION

In 1766, crowds gathered in London to hear the preaching of Samson Occom, a member of the Mohegan Nation of Connecticut Colony. A missionary named Eleazar Wheelock had trained Occom as a Congregational minister. Wheelock sent him to England to raise money for a college in New Hampshire where English and Native American students could study for the ministry. Occom's speaking tour was wildly successful, and he raised much of the money that was needed for the college. In 1769, Wheelock founded Dartmouth College at Hanover. The college enrolled few Native American students, but it became one of the most respected centers for higher learning in the United States. Today, Dartmouth, a member of the Ivy League conference, has strong departments in literature, history, political science, engineering, and many other fields.

The University of New Hampshire began in Hanover in 1866 as an agricultural school called New Hampshire College. The school later moved to Durham. Today, the University System of New Hampshire has campuses in Plymouth, Manchester, Keene, and Durham. About 11,000 undergraduate students pursue degrees in more than 100 fields, including history, creative writing, engineering, business, and environmental science. Graduate degrees are awarded in law, medicine, engineering, computer science, and many other fields.

THINGS OF BEAUTY

The stunning beauty of New Hampshire's landscape has inspired artists since the 19th century. Thomas Cole painted shimmering scenes of the White Mountains, which he visited frequently between 1827 and 1839. Cole is regarded as one of the finest early painters of the United States.

Sculptor Augustus Saint-Gaudens created detailed statues of historical figures. Among them are a statue

MINI-BIO

LAURA BRIDGMAN: LEARNING THROUGH TOUCH

When she was two years old, Laura Bridgman (1829–1889) of Hanover fell ill with a high fever. When her fever came down, her parents were shocked to discover that she had lost her sight and hearing. In 1837, Dr. Samuel Howe heard about Laura and brought her to the Perkins School for the Blind in Boston. Under Howe's direction, the teachers at Perkins taught her to communicate by shaping letters in her hands. She learned to read raised print letters and to write clearly and fluently. Newspapers around the country often ran stories about Laura Bridgman's accomplishments, and people flocked to Perkins to see her. In the 1840s, Bridgman was one of the most famous people in the United States. Though she occasionally visited her family in New Hampshire, she lived at Perkins for the rest of her life. For many years, she taught knitting and needlework to other students at Perkins.

 Want to know more? See http://perkins.pvt.k12.ma.us/museum/section.php?id=213

Sculptor Augustus Saint-Gaudens at work in the late 1800s

Illustrator Maxfield Parrish
in his home, 1950s

of Abraham Lincoln that stands in Chicago's Lincoln Park, and a memorial on Boston Common to Civil War general Robert Shaw and his African American regiment. When he learned that he had cancer in 1900, Saint-Gaudens settled in Cornish on the Connecticut River. Amid the quiet and beauty of the New Hampshire landscape, Saint-Gaudens continued to work, despite his failing health. Soon Cornish became a vibrant community of artists and writers with Saint-Gaudens at its center.

One of the artists who joined Saint-Gaudens in Cornish was illustrator Maxfield Parrish. Parrish illustrated books of fantasy such as *The Arabian Nights* and Nathaniel Hawthorne's

Tanglewood Tales. He was highly successful and painted until the age of 91.

In 1932, a group of New Hampshire craftspeople established the League of New Hampshire Craftsmen Foundation, the first league of its kind in the world. Originally formed to help struggling artisans during the Great Depression, the league now runs a crafts museum in Concord, sponsors a major crafts fair in Newbury, and promotes the teaching and sale of crafts throughout the state.

In 1949, potters Otto Heino and Vivien Place met at a league class. They were married the following year and began to work as a team, known as Otto and Vivika Heino. They always signed their work with both their names, no matter who had been more involved. The Heinos made pots and bowls that are beautiful in their simplicity.

In the 1990s and early 2000s, New Hampshire's artists experimented with new themes and materials. Mary Mead, who teaches at Dartmouth, is a printmaker who also creates abstract sculptures from wood and concrete. Christine Hawkins of Cornish uses wood, ceramic, and fabric to make whimsical pieces. Phil Thorne of Lyme is an environmental scientist who is also dedicated to art. His work uses plastic and other modern materials to explore ancient themes of legend and myth.

JESS BLACKSTONE: BIRDS WERE HIS BUSINESS

As a boy in Melrose, Massachusetts, Jess Blackstone (1909–1988) was fascinated by birds. When he moved to Concord in 1940, he turned his passion into a business. Blackstone carved detailed figures of songbirds, shorebirds, and waterfowl and then painted the carvings in realistic colors. His work sold to collectors all over the world. At the height of his career, he completed two carvings a day.

A vase created by Otto and Vivika Heino

Edward and Marian MacDowell, the visionaries behind the MacDowell Colony

MUSIC IN THE AIR

New Hampshire's English settlers brought a host of ballads, hymns, and popular songs with them from Europe. Later, Scottish and Irish immigrants added reels, jigs, and their own ballads to the medley. The French Canadians who settled in New Hampshire during the 19th century brought their traditional fiddle tunes and dances.

Edward MacDowell grew up in New York and studied music in France and Germany. He was an acclaimed pianist and composer. When he returned to the United States, he and his wife, Marian, bought a summer home near Peterborough. They loved the New Hampshire countryside and

SEE IT HERE!

THE MACDOWELL COLONY

Composer Aaron Copland described the MacDowell Colony as "a place in America where the artist can really work." Scattered across 450 acres (182 hectares) of woodlands and fields near Peterborough are the colony's 32 studios, where some 200 artists, writers, composers, and architects come to work each year. The MacDowell Colony has hosted talents such as composer Leonard Bernstein and writers Willa Cather, James Baldwin, and Alice Walker.

dreamed of creating a place where composers, artists, and writers could come to work and exchange ideas. In 1904, Edward was run over by a horse-drawn cab. He survived the accident but suffered a head injury that destroyed his ability to work. In 1907, Marian founded the MacDowell Colony in Peterborough, a haven of creativity that she and her husband had imagined together.

Writers Philip Roth (right) and William Styron participating in a conference at the MacDowell Colony, 2001

AMY BEACH: MUSICAL GENIUS

When Amy Marcy Cheney Beach (1867–1944) was a small child in Henniker, her parents noticed that she had an astonishing gift for music. When she was a year old, she knew 40 songs. She wrote her first musical pieces when she was four, composing them in her head and then playing them on the piano. Her mother soon took her to Boston, where she studied piano under the finest teachers available. In 1885, she married Dr. Henry Harris Beach, who discouraged her from performing in public. During their years together, Amy Beach composed songs for voice and piano, as well as choral and orchestral music. After her husband's death in 1910, she performed all over the United States and Europe.

? Want to know more? See www.library.unh.edu/special/index.php/amy-beach

ELEANOR HODGMAN PORTER: LOOKING ON THE BRIGHT SIDE

Life was never easy for Eleanor Hodgman Porter (1868–1920) of Littleton. Her father died when she was eight, and her mother became bedridden with a long illness. Eleanor's own health was fragile, and she was not well enough to finish high school. Eventually, she married, moved to Massachusetts, and began to write novels. In 1913, she published *Pollyanna*, the story of a little girl who copes with life's hardships by playing the Glad Game. No matter what happens, Pollyanna tries to find something she can feel glad about. *Pollyanna* was immensely popular. Today, people sometimes say a person has a "Pollyanna attitude" when she or he seems foolishly optimistic.

? Want to know more? See www.golittleton.com/eleanor_porter.php

Poet Celia Laighton Thaxter

TALENTED WRITERS

Today, few people recognize the name Celia Laighton Thaxter, but during the late 19th century, she was one of the most popular poets in the United States. Thaxter grew up on White Island in the Isles of Shoals, where her father was the lighthouse keeper. After she married, she moved with her husband to Newtonville, Massachusetts, but she was never happy there. She continued to spend summers on the Isles of Shoals and described their stark beauty in her poetry. Thaxter's home on Appledore Island attracted a lively group of writers and artists who sang songs, told stories, and enjoyed Thaxter's wit and warmth.

Hundreds of writers have lived and worked in New Hampshire, but poet Robert Frost towers above them all. Frost's poems capture the speech and experiences of the Yankee farmer, and many draw upon his years working a farm in Derry, New Hampshire. Works such as "Mending Wall," "Birches," "Stopping by Woods on a Snowy Evening," and "The Road Not Taken" are among the best-loved poems by any American writer.

Thornton Wilder was among the many writers who worked at the MacDowell Colony. Wilder's 1938 play *Our Town* tells the story of ordinary people living in a fictitious New Hampshire town called Grover's Corners. It is one of the most frequently produced American plays.

J. D. Salinger's novels and short stories have become contemporary classics. His 1951 novel *The Catcher in the Rye* is the story of Holden Caulfield, a 16-year-old boy seeking to escape from a world of "phonies." Today, Salinger lives a private life in Cornish.

More contemporary writers from the state include novelists Robin Cook, John Irving, and Dan Brown.

New Hampshire native Dan Brown wrote the best-seller *The Da Vinci Code.*

The University of New Hampshire women's hockey team prepares for a game in 2006.

In 1931, the Boston and Maine Railroad started to run a special Ski Train from Boston to the slopes at Warner and Conway. Some 60,000 passengers took the Ski Train during its first four years of service.

SPORTS AND RECREATION

New Hampshire has no major league sports teams, so most Granite Staters root for teams from Boston. They cheer on Major League Baseball's Boston Red Sox and the National Football League's New England Patriots. The University of New Hampshire has long had powerhouse men's and women's ice hockey teams. Dartmouth College, a member of the prestigious Ivy League, fields teams for men and women in a variety of sports, including football, soccer, baseball, basketball, ice hockey, track and field, sailing, rowing, and skiing.

Students at Dartmouth were among the first in the United States to experiment with downhill skiing as a sporting event. In 1911, skiing became an important part of Dartmouth's winter carnival. Then, in 1930, a

Franconia innkeeper named Katharine Peckett decided to encourage visitors to come and ski so she could keep her lodge open all winter. She hired two instructors to teach the sport, creating the first ski school in the country.

In addition to skiing, the people of New Hampshire enjoy winter sports such as snowshoeing, sledding, skating, and tobogganing. When the ice and snow disappear, they take to the woods for hiking and camping. Peaks in the White Mountains lure climbers from all over the country.

A biker on the New Hampshire Heritage Trail

JENNY THOMPSON: GOING FOR GOLD

In 1987, Jenny Thompson (1973–) of Dover blasted onto the scene as one of the world's most promising young swimmers after winning the 50-meter freestyle race at the Pan American Games. Thompson swam in her first Olympics in 1992, placing second in the 100-meter freestyle race. Between 1992 and 2004, she won 12 Olympic medals: eight gold, three silver, and one bronze. No other female American athlete has won more Olympic medals. While she was busy being a world-class athlete, she was also getting a world-class education. In 2006, Thompson earned a medical degree from Columbia University.

? Want to know more? See www.newhampshire.com/nh-people/jenny-thompson-biography.aspx

THE NEW HAMPSHIRE HERITAGE TRAIL

In 1988, the New Hampshire legislature launched an ambitious statewide project to create a trail from the Massachusetts border to Canada. The first segment of the New Hampshire Heritage Trail was cut in Franconia Notch State Park. The trail follows the Merrimack River to Franklin and then runs west to the Connecticut River and north to Canada. It offers opportunities for hiking, bicycling, and cross-country skiing.

READ ABOUT

Governor John Lynch joins students on a tour of the capitol in Concord.

CHAPTER SEVEN

GOVERNMENT

★

IN 1977, A GROUP OF FIFTH GRADERS AT BROKEN GROUND ELEMENTARY SCHOOL IN CONCORD CONTACTED THEIR REPRESENTATIVES IN THE NEW HAMPSHIRE LEGISLATURE. They suggested that New Hampshire adopt the ladybug as its state insect. The students collected 100 signatures in support of the idea and sent them to the legislature. Their idea became a bill that was debated in the legislature and finally signed into law by the governor. By proposing a new law and watching the process of its passage, the Concord students learned firsthand about the workings of state government.

Capitol Facts

Here are some fascinating facts about the New Hampshire State House.

- The capitol in Concord was built of granite from quarries at the north end of town. The stones were cut and shaped by inmates of the local prison.
- The legislature met in the new capitol for the first time in 1819.
- Concord's Park Street is named for capitol builder Stuart J. Park.
- Originally, a wooden eagle covered with gold leaf crowned the capitol. After years of being exposed to the New Hampshire weather, the wooden eagle had to be replaced. The new eagle, which is made of metal, is a replica of the original.

THE CONSTITUTION

The New Hampshire Constitution was ratified, or formally approved, in 1784, making it the second-oldest state constitution in the nation. The constitution divides the state government into three separate branches: executive, legislative, and judicial.

The State House in Concord

Capital City

This map shows places of interest in Concord, New Hampshire's capital city.

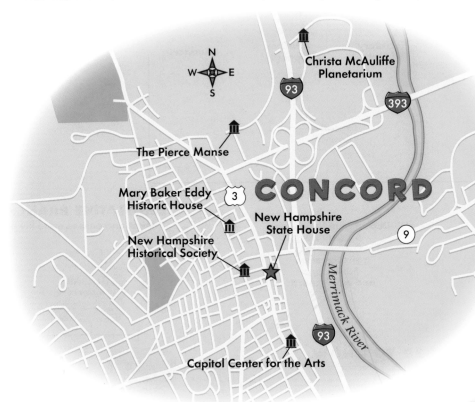

EXECUTIVE BRANCH

The governor of New Hampshire is the state's chief executive. He or she is elected to a two-year term and can be reelected an unlimited number of times. New Hampshire does not have a lieutenant governor to take over if the governor cannot complete his or her term of office. Instead, the governor is assisted by a five-member Executive Council. Members of the Executive Council are elected to two-year terms.

One of the governor's duties is to nominate judges, the attorney general (who represents the state in legal affairs), and the heads of state commissions and

SEE IT HERE!

BRIDGES HOUSE, THE GOVERNOR'S MANSION

Bridges House, New Hampshire's official governor's mansion, was built in Concord in about 1836. Former state governor Styles Bridges bought the house in 1946 and lived there until his death. Under the will of his widow, the house became the official residence of the governor in 1969.

New Hampshire Government

EXECUTIVE BRANCH
Carries out state laws

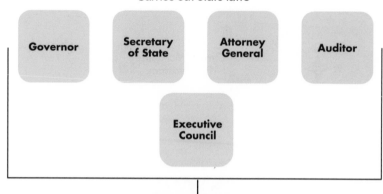

| Governor | Secretary of State | Attorney General | Auditor |

Executive Council

Department heads of:
Agriculture
Corrections
Transportation
Education
and many more

JUDICIAL BRANCH
Enforces state laws

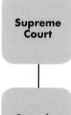

Supreme Court

Superior Court

District Court
(36 members)

Probate Court
(5 counties)

Family Court
(10 members)

WORD TO KNOW

revenue *the money a government receives through taxes and other sources*

LEGISLATIVE BRANCH
Makes and passes state laws

General Court

| Senate (24 members) | House of Representatives (400 members) |

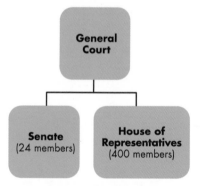

WHERE DOES THE MONEY COME FROM?

It costs a lot of money to run a state government. There are workers to pay, equipment to purchase, and buildings to heat and maintain, to name only a few of the costs New Hampshire faces. Most states pay for their government and its services by collecting a state income tax. New Hampshire is the only state that has neither a general personal income tax nor a sales tax on goods purchased. The state's **revenue** comes from local property taxes, a state lottery, and federal grants. The state's low taxes are attractive to businesses, but the system can put a strain on school budgets and funding for other public programs.

Former New Hampshire governor Craig Benson (right) talks with Senate president Tom Eaton about the state budget in 2003.

agencies, including the Board of Education. These nominees must then be approved by the Executive Council. The governor also has the power to veto a bill that has passed in the state legislature, but the Executive Council can reverse the governor's veto if it wants the bill to become law.

LEGISLATIVE BRANCH

New Hampshire's legislature is called the General Court of New Hampshire, a name it has carried since colonial times. The General Court consists of two chambers, or houses: the house of representatives and the senate. The house of representatives, or lower house, has 400

New Hampshire's legislature is the fourth largest in the world! Only the U.S. Congress and the parliaments of India and Great Britain have more members.

A New Hampshire court in session in Concord

members. Twenty-four members serve in the upper house, or senate. With a total of 424 members, New Hampshire has the biggest legislature of any state in the Union. This contributes to New Hampshirites' high degree of involvement in their state government.

JUDICIAL BRANCH

New Hampshire's court system has several levels. The lowest courts in the state are family courts and probate courts. Family courts handle domestic issues, and probate courts hear cases involving wills and guardianship. District courts handle larger lawsuits of up to $20,000 and also hear some criminal cases. Jury trials are held in the superior courts, which meet in each county. Superior courts handle serious criminal cases, major lawsuits, and divorce cases.

The highest court in New Hampshire is the supreme court. Decisions made in the lower courts can be appealed to the supreme court for a final decision. The supreme court has a chief justice and four associate justices.

DAVID SOUTER: SUPREME COURT JUSTICE

When David Souter (1939–) was 11, his family moved from Massachusetts to a farm in Weare. From that time on, Souter has called New Hampshire his home. After he earned a law degree from Harvard and studied at Oxford University in England, he started a legal practice in Concord. He served as attorney general of New Hampshire from 1976 to 1978. In 1983, he was appointed associate justice on the New Hampshire Supreme Court. President George H. W. Bush appointed Souter to the U.S. Supreme Court in 1990. Souter returns to New Hampshire whenever he gets the chance and loves to hike in the mountains around Weare.

? Want to know more? See www.oyez.org/justices/david_h_souter/

WEIRD LAWS IN NEW HAMPSHIRE

Some pretty strange laws are on the books in New Hampshire. Here are a few, though they are no longer enforced:

- You may not tap your feet or in any way keep time to the music in a tavern or restaurant.
- You are not allowed to sell the clothes you are wearing to pay a gambling debt.
- It is illegal to pick up seaweed on the beach.
- You may not run machinery on Sundays.
- Cows that cross public roads must be fitted with diapers.

Representing New Hampshire

This list shows the number of elected officials who represent New Hampshire, both on the state and national levels.

OFFICE	NUMBER	LENGTH OF TERM
State senators	24	2 years
State representatives	400	2 years
U.S. senators	2	6 years
U.S. representatives	2	2 years
Presidential electors	4	—

FRANKLIN PIERCE: NEW HAMPSHIRE'S PRESIDENT

Born in Hillsborough, Franklin Pierce (1804–1869) was the son of New Hampshire governor Benjamin Pierce. Franklin Pierce earned a law degree and worked for a time in Concord before he was drawn into politics. He won a seat in the U.S. Congress in 1832 and became a U.S. senator in 1837. He ran for president in 1852, at a time when the issue of slavery divided the country. He became the 14th U.S. president, elected as a moderate who opposed slavery but wanted to have smooth relations with the South. A few weeks before Pierce moved into the White House, his 12-year-old son Benny was killed in a train accident. Pierce's presidency was shadowed by gloom, and his efforts to heal the nation's wounds were unsuccessful.

 Want to know more? See www.whitehouse.gov/history/presidents/fp14.html

LOCAL GOVERNMENT

New Hampshire is divided into 10 counties. People in each county elect officials including a county sheriff, county commissioners, and a registrar of deeds who keeps records on the ownership of property.

The state's 221 incorporated towns are sometimes referred to as "little republics" because they exercise a form of direct democracy. Since colonial days, citizens of each town have gathered on the second Tuesday in March for an annual town meeting. At these meetings, people discuss local issues and concerns. They elect town officials and vote on taxes, budgets, and policies. This keeps government close to the people.

In 1996, the New Hampshire legislature created another option for towns to transact their business, known as the SB2 form of government. The term SB2 comes from the New Hampshire senate bill that made this option into law. Under SB2, instead of meeting face-to-face, townspeople go to a polling place to vote on many issues and to elect town officials. By 2005, about 25 percent of New Hampshire towns had switched to the SB2 form of government. Many New Hampshirites think that the SB2 method is more in keeping with the busy lifestyle of the 21st century. They argue that few

New Hampshire Counties

This map shows the 10 counties in New Hampshire. Concord, the state capital, is indicated with a star.

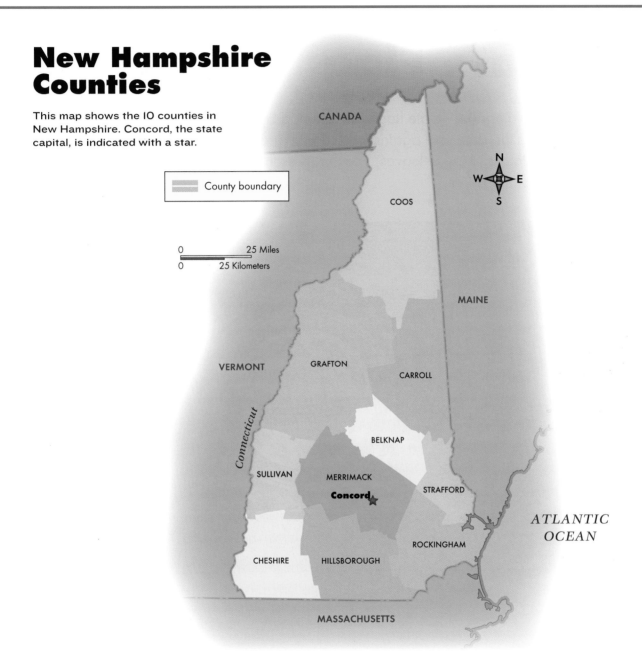

people can afford to spend hours at a meeting. They prefer to acquaint themselves with the issues on their own time and vote quickly and efficiently. Many others, however, miss the spirited debate that takes place in town meetings.

State Flag

New Hampshire's state flag was adopted by the state legislature in 1909. It depicts the state seal against a blue background. The seal is surrounded by nine stars and laurel leaves, which represent New Hampshire being the ninth state of the Union.

State Seal

New Hampshire's first state seal was created in 1775. It featured a pine tree, fish, and a set of five arrows representing the five counties then in New Hampshire. As time went on, the state legislature decided that the seal needed to be changed in order to accurately represent the state's strengths. In 1931, the current state seal design was adopted. The seal features one of the nation's first naval ships, the *Raleigh*, which was built in Portsmouth. This represents New Hampshire's strong shipbuilding industry. The date on the bottom of the seal reads 1776, in honor of the year the United States declared its independence. The seal also shows the sun rising over the Atlantic Ocean and a circle of laurel leaves.

98

READ ABOUT

A hotel clerk uses a map to give directions in the town of Ashland.

CHAPTER EIGHT

ECONOMY

★

WORKERS REPAIR A SUBMARINE AT THE PORTSMOUTH NAVAL SHIPYARD. Farmhands operate a milking machine on a dairy farm in the Connecticut Valley. In the White Mountains, a guide leads a group of visitors along a rocky trail. All of these people are involved in New Hampshire's workforce. Like many thousands of others, they contribute to New Hampshire's economy.

A social worker checks in with nurses at a New Hampshire retirement home.

WORD TO KNOW

gross state product *the total value of all the goods and services produced in a state*

DOING THINGS FOR OTHERS

People who work in the service industries do not make items to sell or grow crops. Instead, they provide services for others. Service industries account for the largest part of New Hampshire's **gross state product** (GSP).

People who repair computers provide a service, as do doctors, lawyers, teachers, hairstylists, store clerks, and innkeepers. Those employed by banks and insurance companies are also part of the service industries. Most of these businesses are concentrated in the southern part of the state, especially in Manchester, Nashua, and Concord. People who work for the government are also part of the service sector. This includes the men and women who work at the Portsmouth Naval Shipyard, because they are employed by the U.S. Navy.

MAKING THINGS

Until the 1920s, the textile industry was the mainstay of New Hampshire's manufacturing economy. The mills have now disappeared, and New Hampshire is deeply involved in a different industry: electronics. Plants in Nashua, Rochester, and Salem make microchips and networking systems. New Hampshire also produces communication systems used by the military.

SEE IT HERE!

PORTSMOUTH NAVAL SHIPYARD

Portsmouth has been a center of the shipbuilding industry since colonial times. Today, as one of only four remaining naval shipyards in the nation, Portsmouth overhauls, maintains, and repairs nuclear-powered submarines for the U.S. Navy. About 3,900 highly skilled workers handle assignments that may take from a few days to two years to complete. On the grounds of the shipyard is a memorial to the lost crew members of the Portsmouth submarine USS *Squalus*. Twenty-six men died when the submarine sank off the Isles of Shoals in 1939.

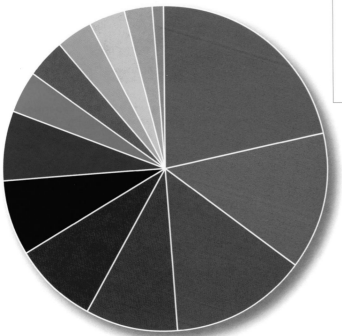

What Do New Hampshirites Do?

This color-coded chart shows what industries New Hampshirites work in.

21.8% Educational services, health care, and social assistance, 153,310

13.7% Manufacturing, 96,511

13.7% Retail trade, 96,495

9.2% Professional, scientific, management, administrative, and waste management services, 65,027

8.4% Construction, 59,218

7.6% Arts, entertainment, recreation, accommodation, and food services, 53,432

6.8% Finance, insurance, real estate, rental, and leasing, 48,236

4.4% Other services, except public administration, 30,845

3.7% Public administration, 26,359

3.7% Transportation, warehousing, and utilities, 26,147

3.6% Wholesale trade, 25,461

2.6% Information, 18,374

0.8% Agriculture, forestry, fishing, hunting, and mining, 5,359

Source: U.S. Census Bureau, 2006 estimate

The lumber industry remains an important part of New Hampshire's economy.

| MINI-BIO |

DEAN KAMEN: INVENTOR

Dean Kamen (1951–) has always been a problem solver. He has more than 440 inventions to his name, including a water purification system, an all-terrain electric wheelchair, and many robotic devices. In 2001, he invented a computer-driven human transporter called the Segway. To encourage young inventors, Kamen founded an organization called FIRST (For Invention and Recognition of Science and Technology). Each year, hundreds of high school students team up with professional robotics engineers at the FIRST National Robotics Competition. Winners of the competition are invited to visit Kamen's mansion in Bedford.

❓ Want to know more? See www.invent.org/hall_of_fame/222.html

Factories in the Granite State produce metal products such as ball bearings, braces, and support beams. They also make telecommunications cables, machinery for grinding lenses, and equipment used in the printing and metal industries.

PRODUCTS FROM THE LAND

Only about 8 percent of New Hampshire's land is devoted to agriculture. Though the state has more than 3,000 farms, most of them are relatively small. Leading farm products come from nurseries and include garden flowers, ornamental bushes, and Christmas trees. Hay is the state's leading field crop, and sweet corn is its top vegetable. New Hampshire's orchards are noted for their apples.

The rich grasses of the Connecticut River valley provide fine pasture for New Hampshire's dairy herds. New Hampshire farms also produce beef cattle, hogs, and eggs.

Top Products

Agriculture	Greenhouse/nursery, dairy products, apples, cattle, corn, hay, chicken eggs, maple products, aquaculture, hogs, turkeys
Manufacturing	Machinery, electric equipment, rubber, plastic products
Mining	Sand, gravel, clay, granite

The first potatoes grown in the American colonies were planted at Londonderry in 1719.

Picking beans at a family farm in the southern part of the state

New Hampshire granite is used for kitchen counters like these, as well as for buildings, statues, and monuments throughout the country.

FAQ

Q: ARE ANY GEMSTONES FOUND IN NEW HAMPSHIRE?

A: Yes. Several gemstones are found in New Hampshire, including amethyst, apatite, garnet, smoky quartz, and topaz. They are not mined commercially, but amateur collectors sometimes use them for making jewelry.

FROM MINES AND QUARRIES

Stones in New Hampshire's fields have always been a challenge to farmers, but stone is also a profitable product. The Granite State has active quarries where workers remove granite blocks for building and crushed stone for roadbeds and concrete. Hillsborough and Merrimack counties are leading producers of sand and gravel used in the construction business.

Major Agricultural and Mining Products

This map shows where New Hampshire's major agricultural and mining products come from. See a milk carton? That means dairy products are made there.

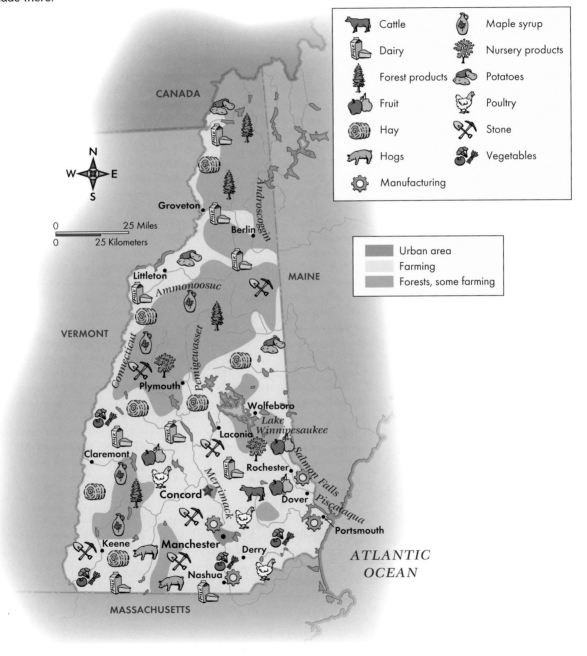

CANADA

MAINE

VERMONT

MASSACHUSETTS

ATLANTIC
OCEAN

95 Interstate highway

0   25 Miles
0   25 Kilometers

N
W   E
S

Groveton

Berlin

Lancaster

Androscoggin

Sargent's Purchase

North
Conway

Franconia

Franconia
Notch

Lincoln

93

Holderness

Plymouth

Moultonborough

Hanover

Ashland

Geographic Center of
New Hampshire

Wolfeboro

*Lake
Winnipesaukee*

Cornish

Grafton

Franklin

Laconia

Salmon Falls

Milton

Claremont

89

Canterbury

Rochester

Merrimack

Concord

Charlestown

Allenstown

Dover

Piscataqua

Hillsborough

Candia

Portsmouth

Exeter

95

Keene

Manchester

Auburn

Rye

93

Derry

Hampton

Milford

Jaffrey

Londonderry

Salem

Rindge

Nashua

Connecticut

CHAPTER NINE

TRAVEL GUIDE

TRAVEL GUIDE

★

WITH ITS SOARING MOUNTAINS, BRILLIANT LAKES, BUSTLING CITIES, AND CUTE VILLAGES, NEW HAMPSHIRE IS A MAGNET FOR VISITORS. The Granite State offers a host of outdoor delights for every season: birding in the spring, hiking and camping in the summer, viewing the magnificently colored leaves in the fall, and skiing in the winter. In the Granite State, there is something for everyone!

← Follow along with this travel map. We'll begin in Salem and end our trip in Franconia.

SEACOAST

THINGS TO DO: Ride an antique merry-go-round, go eye to eye with a lobster, and discover how colonial people lived at Strawbery Banke.

Salem

★ **Canobie Lake Park:** This amusement park opened in 1902, and it's still popular today. Ride an antique merry-go-round or take your pick of the four roller coasters. On a hot summer day, the log flume water ride is just the thing!

SEE IT HERE!

AMERICA'S STONEHENGE

One of the most mysterious spots in the United States, America's Stonehenge in Salem is a maze of human-made walls and chambers built some 4,000 years ago. The site is named after Stonehenge, a site in England where people thousands of years ago set massive stones in a circle. Scientists studying America's Stonehenge discovered that the sun casts shadows among the walls at certain times of the year, so that the structure serves as a kind of calendar. The people who built it had an advanced knowledge of astronomy. No one knows who they were or why they created these stoneworks on the New Hampshire seacoast.

Exeter

★ **American Independence Museum:** This museum focuses on the role of New Hampshire in the American Revolution and the building of the new nation.

Portsmouth

★ **Strawbery Banke Museum:** On 9.5 acres (3.8 ha) near the Piscataqua River stand buildings representing four centuries of Portsmouth history. On display are tools, household items, and other artifacts from the original Strawbery Banke settlement.

★ **Wentworth-Coolidge Mansion:** Benning Wentworth, royal governor of New Hampshire from 1741 to 1767, had this mansion constructed for himself. Today, the mansion has been restored, and the carriage house is a visitors' center.

★ **Prescott Park:** This popular waterfront park is the site of a summer arts festival and boasts extensive flower gardens.

Prescott Park

★ **Seacoast African American Cultural Center:** This unique museum celebrates the lives and achievements of African Americans, especially those in the Seacoast community. Besides offering exhibits on African American history in coastal New England, the center also hosts lectures and concerts.

Visitors viewing crabs at the Seacoast Science Center

Rye

★ **Seacoast Science Center:** Located in Odiorne Point State Park, the center provides programs that teach about tides, ocean minerals, and the plants and animals of the seashore. Visitors can get a close-up look at lobsters, horseshoe crabs, and other sea creatures. They can even feel some creatures in the touch tank.

MERRIMACK VALLEY

THINGS TO DO: Attend a poetry reading at the Robert Frost Farm, watch fish swim upstream, and hurtle down a giant waterslide.

FAQ

Q: WHO WERE THE SHAKERS?

A: The Shakers were members of a religious group who chose to live apart from the rest of the world in self-sustaining communities. They believed in a life of simplicity, dedicated to prayer and service to God.

Canterbury

★ **Canterbury Shaker Village:** Once the site of a thriving religious community, this national historic landmark includes 25 fully restored Shaker buildings and four others that have been reconstructed. The Shakers were known for making beautiful furniture, and you can see how it was built at workshops on the grounds.

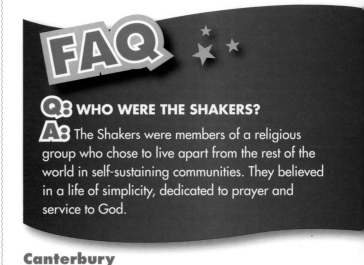

Canterbury Shaker Village

Derry

★ **Robert Frost Farm:** Poet Robert Frost and his family lived in this simple white farmhouse from 1900 to 1911. Many of Frost's greatest poems were inspired by his years here. Today, the house is open to visitors. For a special treat, drop by for one of the poetry readings that are held regularly at the house.

Manchester

★ **Amoskeag Fishways:** Vast numbers of fish used to migrate up the Merrimack every spring to lay their eggs in freshwater. Although their numbers are much smaller now, some shad, salmon, alewives, and other fish still make their way up the river. Human-made **fish ladders** help them swim over dams in the river. At the Amoskeag Fishways, you can watch their progress through underwater windows. The museum offers a variety of programs on river ecology that show the impact of human activity.

WORD TO KNOW

fish ladders *series of pools that allow fish to swim over the tops of dams*

★ **Lawrence L. Lee Scouting Museum:** At this museum, you will find one of the world's biggest collections of Boy Scout memorabilia. Trace more than a century of Boy Scout history in New Hampshire, across the United States, and around the world.

★ **Millyard Museum:** This museum traces 11,000 years of the region's history, beginning with the Native people who camped and fished along the Merrimack. Many of the museum's exhibits center on the lives of the millworkers at the Amoskeag factory. The museum is housed in one of the factory complex's original buildings.

★ **Currier Museum of Art:** Painting and sculpture from Europe and the United States are on display at this renowned art museum. Among the museum's treasures are works by great painters such as Pablo Picasso, Georgia O'Keeffe, and Alexander Calder. The museum also includes works by New England artists.

Robert Frost's mailbox

★ **Zimmerman House:** Architect Frank Lloyd Wright designed this house in 1950. He also designed what went inside the house, including its furniture, draperies, and even its mailbox. A visit to the house is a glimpse into family life in the 1950s and 1960s. This is the only house in New England designed by Wright that is open to the public.

Concord

★ **Pierce Manse:** Franklin Pierce owned this house between 1842 and 1848, before he became president. In 1971, the house was moved from its original site nearby and fully restored.

★ **Christa McAuliffe Planetarium:** This planetarium was named for the New Hampshire teacher who lost her life in the space shuttle *Challenger* explosion. The slogan here is, "The sky is no limit, it is just the beginning." Take part in a rocket-building workshop, study the stars through a high-powered telescope, and learn about the place of our planet in the solar system.

★ **New Hampshire Historical Society's museum:** This museum examines the state's heritage from colonial days to the present.

Ongoing exhibits include an original Concord stagecoach, a reconstructed wigwam, and a fire tower.

New Hampshire Historical Society's museum

SEE IT HERE!

THE MYSTERY STONE

In 1872, workers digging near Lake Winnipesaukee found a buried lump of clay with a strange oval stone inside. The stone was covered with markings that appear to have been carved by human hands. Since the stone's discovery, scientists have debated about who carved it and what its symbols mean. The Mystery Stone is one of the most popular attractions at the New Hampshire Historical Society's museum.

Mystery Stone

Auburn

★ **Massabesic Audubon Center:**
Bring your binoculars and walk
the trails that thread through
the center's bird sanctuary. If
you're patient, you may catch a
glimpse of the ospreys that nest on
Massabesic Lake.

Allenstown

★ **Museum of Family Camping:**
Camping became a popular family
activity late in the 19th century. At
this museum, you can see camping
equipment that was used more than
100 years ago. On display are an
1895 sleeping bag (it weighs 10 times
more than the modern version) and
tent trailers from the 1930s.

Candia

★ **Liquid Planet:** Relax, cool off, and
have fun at this water park. The
magnificent Fountain of Youth is
filled with slides, floats, and other
water rides. If you're especially
daring, try the Time Warp, a 272-
foot (83 m) waterslide that will
make you feel as if you've splashed
into another dimension.

SOUTHWEST

**THINGS TO DO: Climb Mount
Monadnock, visit Franklin
Pierce's boyhood home, or
relax in a serene pine forest.**

Jaffrey

★ **Monadnock State Park:** This
lovely park is a great place for
hiking, picnicking, and camping.
Climbing Mount Monadnock has
been a popular outing since the
late 19th century.

**Mount Monadnock is the second-
most frequently climbed mountain
in the world. Only Mount Fuji in
Japan is climbed more often.**

Hillsborough

★ **Franklin Pierce Homestead:** This
is the childhood home of the 14th
U.S. president. The Pierces were
a well-to-do family, and the house
reflects their high social standing. A
magnificent ballroom for entertain-
ing in grand style runs the length of
the second floor.

Keene

★ **Horatio Colony Museum:** In the
1890s, this was the summer home
of naturalist Horatio Colony. He
set aside the surrounding land as a

wildlife sanctuary. Today, it offers a variety of exhibits and programs on local plants and wildlife.

Rindge

★ **Cathedral of the Pines:** Open to people of all faiths, this "cathedral without walls" in a pine forest is dedicated to the men and women who have given their lives in the fight for freedom and to those who have served the cause of peace.

LAKE COUNTRY AND CONNECTICUT VALLEY

THINGS TO DO: Take a scenic tram ride, talk to a colonial soldier, and explore glacial caves.

Charlestown

★ **The Fort at No. 4 Living History Museum:** English settlers built the Fort at No. 4 in the 1740s to protect themselves from attack. Today, guides in period costumes portray soldiers and colonists. As you experience the daily life of the fort, you can churn butter, play early American games, or trade with visiting Indian trappers.

Moultonborough

★ **Castle in the Clouds:** Enjoy hiking, horseback riding, and a scenic tram ride through the sprawling 5,400-acre (2,185 ha) Castle Springs Estate.

Grafton

★ **The Mine in the Sky:** If you're a rock hound, you won't want to miss this spot! It's the oldest mica, feldspar, and beryl mine in the nation, and you're welcome to have at it with your pick and trowel.

Hanover

★ **Hood Museum of Art:** As you step into this art museum on the Dartmouth College campus, you will see exhibits of work by some of the college's most talented students. Permanent collections include works by artists in Africa, Europe, the Americas, and Asia.

The Fort at No. 4 Living History Museum

Statue of Abraham Lincoln on display at Saint-Gaudens National Historic Site

Cornish

★ **Saint-Gaudens National Historic Site:** Explore Aspet, the home of sculptor Augustus Saint-Gaudens. Galleries display 100 of his original pieces, including models for U.S. gold coins that were minted early in the 20th century.

Claremont

★ **Claremont Historical Society Museum:** This museum features exhibits related to the history of the Claremont region.

Holderness

★ **Squam Lakes Natural Science Center:** Learn about New Hampshire wildlife through live animal exhibits and cruises on the lake. The center sponsors a variety of educational programs.

Ashland

★ **Gliddon Toy Museum:** Antique dolls, ingenious windup toys, challenging games—this museum displays more than 2,000 toys from the 19th and early 20th centuries.

Plymouth

★ **Polar Caves Park:** Self-guided tours let you explore a series of caves created by the great glaciers that once covered New Hampshire.

Milton

★ **New Hampshire Farm Museum:** Three centuries of rural life are on view at the Jones Farmhouse, the Plummer homestead, and a three-story barn.

Wolfeboro

★ **New Hampshire Boat Museum:** A group of vintage boat enthusiasts founded this museum in 1992 to preserve the heritage of lake and river boating in New Hampshire. On display are early motor-powered boats, canoes, models, photos, and sailing and rowing trophies.

★ **Wright Museum:** If World War II fascinates you, don't miss this museum. The centerpiece is an extensive display of tanks, military jeeps, and other wartime vehicles.

NORTH COUNTRY

THINGS TO DO: Ride a train up a mountainside, watch bears shoot hoops, and learn how maple sugar is made.

Sargent's Purchase

★ **Mount Washington:** Get your gear and hike the highest peak in the northeastern United States. But check the weather report first. The winds can be brutal!

North Conway

★ **Conway Scenic Railroad:** From the station in North Conway, you can take your choice of scenic train rides. The Notch Train and the Valley Train are both diesel powered. The steam-powered 7470 makes an excursion from North Conway to Conway.

Lincoln

★ **Clark's Trading Post:** At this roadside attraction, four generations of the Clark family have been training black bears since 1949. Watch the bears shoot hoops, climb poles, and swing on swings. The museum on the grounds includes oddities such as a stuffed two-headed calf born in 1944.

Groveton

★ **Graymist Farm:** To learn more about modern farming techniques, visit Graymist Farm. Tour the vegetable fields, flour operations, and dairy barn. For a treat, try their homemade ice cream!

Lancaster

★ **Christies' Maple Farm and Maple Museum:** Take a self-guided tour through the museum and surrounding orchards. See how maple sugar is processed from raw sap, and buy a jug of fresh maple syrup to carry home with you.

Franconia

★ **New England Ski Museum:** Watch the masters of skiing swoop downhill in a series of continuously running documentary films. Exhibits cover the history of skiing in New Hampshire and throughout the world.

New England Ski Museum

WRITING PROJECTS

Check out these ideas for creating a campaign brochure and writing you-are-there narratives. Or research the lives of famous people from the state.

118

ART PROJECTS

You can illustrate the state song, create a dazzling PowerPoint presentation, or learn about the state quarter and design your own.

119

TIMELINE

What happened when? This timeline highlights important events in the state's history—and shows what was happening throughout the United States at the same time.

122

FAST FACTS

Use this section to find fascinating facts about state symbols, land area and population statistics, weather, sports teams, and much more.

126

GLOSSARY

Remember the Words to Know from the chapters in this book? They're all collected here.

125

SCIENCE, TECHNOLOGY, & MATH PROJECTS

Make weather maps, graph population statistics, and research endangered species that live in the state.

120

PRIMARY VS. SECONDARY SOURCES

121

So what are primary and secondary sources? And what's the diff? This section explains all that and where you can find them.

133

BIOGRAPHICAL DICTIONARY

This at-a-glance guide highlights some of the state's most important and influential people. Visit this section and read about their contributions to the state, the country, and the world.

RESOURCES

Books, Web sites, DVDs, and more. Take a look at these additional sources for information about the state.

137

WRITING PROJECTS

★ ★ ★

Write a Memoir, Journal, or Editorial for Your School Newspaper!

Picture Yourself . . .

★ In an Abenaki sugar camp. It's early spring, and snow is still on the ground. The grown-ups have been watching the moon and the weather. They know it's time to go sugaring. What would life be like living with your family in the sugar camp?

SEE: Chapter Two, pages 27–28.
GO TO: www.umext.maine.edu/onlinepubs/pdfpubs/7036.pdf

★ On your way to fight the British army during the Revolutionary War. What and whom would you be fighting for, and what hardships would you endure on the battlefield?

SEE: Chapter Three, pages 43–44.
GO TO: www.vancortlandthouse.org/Soldier%20in%20the%20Revolutionary%20War.htm

Create an Election Brochure or Web Site!

Run for office! Throughout this book, you've read about some of the issues that concern New Hampshire today. As a candidate for governor of New Hampshire, create a campaign brochure or Web site.

★ Explain how you meet the qualifications to be governor of New Hampshire.

★ Talk about the three or four major issues you'll focus on if you're elected.

★ Remember, you'll be responsible for New Hampshire's budget. What programs would you approve money for?

SEE: Chapter Seven, pages 89–91.

GO TO: New Hampshire's government Web site at www.nh.gov. You might also want to check out some local newspapers. Try these:

Concord Monitor at www.concordmonitor.com

New Hampshire Union Leader (Manchester) at www.theunionleader.com

Telegraph (Nashua) at www.nashuatelegraph.com

Create an interview script with a famous person from New Hampshire!

★ Research various New Hampshirites, such as Passaconaway, Daniel Webster, Harriet Dame, Christa McAuliffe, Robert Frost, Jenny Thompson, or Jeanne Shaheen.

★ Based on your research, pick one person you would most like to talk with.

★ Write a script of the interview. What questions would you ask? How would this person answer? Create a question-and-answer format. You may want to supplement this writing project with a voice-recording dramatization of the interview.

SEE: Chapters Three, Four, Five, Six, and Seven, pages 38, 53, 54, 66, 82, 83, and 85, and the Biographical Dictionary, pages 133–136.

GO TO: www.concord.k12.nh.us/schools/kimball/leduc/nhhist2.htm

ART PROJECTS

★ ★ ★

Create a PowerPoint Presentation or Visitors' Guide

Welcome to New Hampshire!

New Hampshire's a great place to visit and to live! From its natural beauty to its historical sites, there's plenty to see and do. In your PowerPoint presentation or brochure, highlight 10 to 15 of New Hampshire's fascinating landmarks. Be sure to include:

★ a map of the state showing where these sites are located

★ photos, illustrations, Web links, natural history facts, geographic stats, climate and weather, plants and wildlife, and recent discoveries

SEE: Chapter Nine, pages 106–115, and Fast Facts, pages 126–127.

GO TO: The official tourism Web site for New Hampshire at www.visitnh.gov.

Download and print maps, photos, and vacation ideas for tourists.

Illustrate the Lyrics to the New Hampshire State Song

("Old New Hampshire")

Use markers, paints, photos, collages, colored pencils, or computer graphics to illustrate the lyrics to "Old New Hampshire." Turn your illustrations into a picture book, or scan them into PowerPoint and add music.

SEE: The lyrics to "Old New Hampshire" on page 128.

GO TO: The New Hampshire state government Web site at www.nh.gov to find out more about the origin of the state song.

State Quarter Project

From 1999 to 2008, the U.S. Mint introduced new quarters commemorating each of the 50 states in the order that they were admitted to the Union. Each state's quarter features a unique design on its back, or reverse.

GO TO: www.usmint.gov/kids and find out what's featured on the back of the New Hampshire quarter.

★ Research the significance of the image. Who designed the quarter? Who chose the final design?

★ Design your own New Hampshire quarter. What images would you choose for the reverse?

★ Make a poster showing the New Hampshire quarter and label each image.

SCIENCE, TECHNOLOGY, & MATH PROJECTS

★ ★ ★

Graph Population Statistics!

★ Compare population statistics (such as ethnic background, birth, death, and literacy rates) in New Hampshire counties or major cities.

★ In your graph or chart, look at population density and write sentences describing what the population statistics show; graph one set of population statistics and write a paragraph explaining what the graphs reveal.

SEE: Chapter Six, pages 70–73.

GO TO: The official Web site for the U.S. Census Bureau at www.census.gov and at http://quickfacts.census.gov/qfd/states/33000.html to find out more about population statistics, how they work, and what the statistics are for New Hampshire.

Create a Weather Map of New Hampshire!

Use your knowledge of New Hampshire's geography to research and identify conditions that result in specific weather events. What is it about the geography of New Hampshire that makes it vulnerable to blizzards? Create a weather map or poster that shows the weather patterns over the state. Include a caption explaining the technology used to measure weather phenomena and provide data.

SEE: Chapter One, page 16.

GO TO: The National Oceanic and Atmospheric Administration's National Weather Service Web site at www.weather.gov for weather maps and forecasts for New Hampshire.

Karner blue butterfly

Track Endangered Species

Using your knowledge of New Hampshire's wildlife, research which animals and plants are endangered or threatened.

★ Find out what the state is doing to protect these species.

★ Chart known populations of the animals and plants, and report on changes in certain geographic areas.

SEE: Chapter One, page 21.

GO TO: Web sites such as www.fws.gov/northeast/Endangered/ for lists of endangered species in New Hampshire.

PRIMARY VS. SECONDARY SOURCES

★ ★ ★

What's the Diff?

Your teacher may require at least one or two primary sources and one or two secondary sources for your assignment. So, what's the difference between the two?

★ **Primary sources are original.** You are reading the actual words of someone's diary, journal, letter, autobiography, or interview. Primary sources can also be photographs, maps, prints, cartoons, news/film footage, posters, first-person newspaper articles, drawings, musical scores, and recordings. By the way, when you conduct a survey, interview someone, shoot a video, or take photographs to include in a project, you are creating primary sources!

★ **Secondary sources are what you find in encyclopedias, textbooks, articles, biographies, and almanacs.** These are written by a person or group of people who tell about something that happened to someone else. Secondary sources also recount what another person said or did. This book is an example of a secondary source.

Now that you know what primary sources are—where can you find them?

★ **Your school or local library:** Check the library catalog for collections of original writings, government documents, musical scores, and so on. Some of this material may be stored on microfilm. The Library of Congress Web site (www.loc.gov) is an excellent online resource for primary source materials.

★ **Historical societies:** These organizations keep historical documents, photographs, and other materials. Staff members can help you find what you are looking for. History museums are also great places to see primary sources firsthand.

★ **The Internet:** There are lots of sites that have primary sources you can download and use in a project or assignment.

TIMELINE

★ ★ ★

U.S. Events | **8000 BCE** | **New Hampshire Events**

8000 BCE
The first people enter present-day New Hampshire.

1000 BCE

1000 BCE
People live in settled villages, beginning the Woodland Period.

Remains of a Woodland pot

1400

1492
Christopher Columbus and his crew sight land in the Caribbean Sea.

1500

1565
Spanish admiral Pedro Menéndez de Avilés founds St. Augustine, Florida, the oldest continuously occupied European settlement in the continental United States.

Late 1500s CE
Several Native groups come together to form the Pennacook Nation.

1600

1607
The first permanent English settlement in North America is established at Jamestown.

1616-19
An epidemic kills more than 90 percent of the Native people in what is now New Hampshire.

1614
John Smith leads an expedition up the New England coast and stops at the Isles of Shoals.

1620
Pilgrims found Plymouth Colony, the second permanent English settlement.

1622
John Mason receives a large land grant in what is now New Hampshire.

1641
Scattered settlements in present-day New Hampshire join the Massachusetts Bay Colony.

1682
René-Robert Cavelier, Sieur de La Salle, claims more than 1 million square miles (2.6 million sq km) of territory in the Mississippi River basin for France, naming it Louisiana.

U.S. Events

New Hampshire Events

1691
New Hampshire becomes a separate colony.

1700

1754
Robert Rogers forms Rogers' Rangers
to attack the French in Canada.

1776
Thirteen American colonies declare their
independence from Great Britain.

1787
The U.S. Constitution is written.

1788
New Hampshire ratifies the U.S.
Constitution, becoming the ninth state.

1800

1803
The Louisiana Purchase almost doubles
the size of the United States.

1808
Concord becomes New Hampshire's capital.

1820s
Textile mills open in many New
Hampshire towns, employing thousands
of girls and young women.

1830
The Indian Removal Act forces eastern
Native American groups to relocate
west of the Mississippi River.

1832
Settlers in northern New Hampshire
establish the Republic of Indian Stream.

1846–48
The United States fights a war with Mexico
over western territories in the Mexican War.

1852
Franklin Pierce of Hillsborough is
elected the 14th U.S. president.

1861–65
The American Civil War is fought
between the Northern Union and the
Southern Confederacy; it ends with
the surrender of the Confederate army,
led by General Robert E. Lee.

1880s
The Boston and Maine Railroad gains control
of the New Hampshire railroad industry.

1890s
The Amoskeag
Manufacturing Company
is the world's biggest
producer of cotton cloth.

1898
The United States gains control of
Cuba, Puerto Rico, the Philippines,
and Guam after defeating Spain
in the Spanish-American War.

Amoskeag Manufacturing Company

U.S. Events `1900` **New Hampshire Events**

1911
New Hampshire passes a strong
law limiting child labor.

1917–18
The United States engages in World War I.

1922
Workers at the Amoskeag Manufacturing
Company go on strike.

1929
The stock market crashes, plunging the United
States more deeply into the Great Depression.

1941–45
The United States engages in World War II.

1941–45
The Portsmouth Naval Shipyard builds
hundreds of vessels during World War II.

1944
The International Monetary Conference
meets at Bretton Woods.

1951–53
The United States engages in the Korean War.

1964–73
The United States engages in the Vietnam War.

1974
New Hampshirites defeat a proposal
by Aristotle Onassis to build the world's
largest oil refinery in Durham.

1990
A nuclear power plant opens at Seabrook
after a 17-year battle with environmentalists.

1991
The United States and other nations engage
in the brief Persian Gulf War against Iraq.

1996
`2000` Jeanne Shaheen is elected New
Hampshire's first female governor.

2001
Terrorists attack the United
States on September 11.

2003
The United States and coalition
forces invade Iraq.

2003
New Hampshire's symbol,
the Old Man of the Mountain,
collapses.

Jeanne Shaheen

2008
The United States elects its first African
American president, Barack Obama.

GLOSSARY

★ ★ ★

anadromous fish fish that spend most of their lives in salt water but breed in freshwater

brackish slightly salty

breechcloths garments worn by men over their lower bodies

canneries factories where food is canned

effigy a figure of a person or animal

eskers fields of jagged, protruding rocks

famines periods of extreme food shortages and hunger

fish ladders series of pools that allow fish to swim over the tops of dams

gross state product the total value of all the goods and services produced in a state

guerrilla a soldier who doesn't belong to a regular army; guerrillas often use surprise attacks and other uncommon battle tactics

immunity protection against disease

metamorphic describing rocks that have been changed by extreme pressure, wind, and water

militia an army made up of citizens trained to serve as soldiers in an emergency

monadnocks giant outcrops of rock that did not wear away as surrounding rock was ground down

monopolies companies that control the entire supply of a particular good or service

precipitation all water that falls to the earth, including rain, sleet, hail, snow, dew, fog, or mist

privateers private citizens given government approval to capture enemy ships

redcoats British soldiers, especially during the American Revolution

repealed withdrew, undid

republic a nation in which citizens can vote; republics are usually led by presidents

revenue the money a government receives through taxes and other sources

seceded withdrew from a group or an organization

selectman an official elected to help run a New England town

strike an organized refusal to work, usually as a sign of protest about working conditions

Tories people who remained loyal to the British during the American Revolution

tundra treeless plain

underground railroad a secret network of people who helped those fleeing slavery reach freedom

FAST FACTS

★ ★ ★

State Symbols

State seal

Statehood date	June 21, 1788; the 9th state
Origin of state name	Named in 1629 by Captain John Mason of Plymouth Council for New England after his home county of Hampshire, England
State capital	Concord
State nickname	Granite State
State motto	"Live Free or Die"
State bird	Purple finch
State flower	Purple lilac
State insect	Ladybug
State amphibian	Spotted newt
State butterfly	Karner blue
State saltwater game fish	Striped bass
State freshwater fish	Brook trout
State rock	Granite
State mineral	Beryl
State gem	Smoky quartz
State song	"Old New Hampshire" (this is the official state song; there are eight honorary state songs)
State tree	White birch
State wildflower	Pink lady's slipper

Geography

Total area; rank	9,350 square miles (24,216 sq km); 46th
Land; rank	8,968 square miles (23,227 sq km); 44th
Water; rank	382 square miles (989 sq km); 45th
Inland water; rank	314 square miles (813 sq km); 44th
Territorial water; rank	68 square miles (176 sq km); 22nd
Geographic center	Belknap, 3 miles (5 km) east of Ashland
Latitude	42°40' N to 45°18' N
Longitude	70°37' W to 72°37' W
Highest point	Mount Washington, 6,288 feet (1,917 m), located in Coos County
Lowest point	Sea level, at the Atlantic Ocean

Largest city Manchester
Longest river Connecticut

Population

Population; rank (2007 estimate) 1,315,828; 41st
Density (2007 estimate) 147 persons per square mile (57 per sq km)
Population distribution (2000 census) 59% urban, 41% rural
Race (2007 estimate) White persons: 95.6%*

Asian persons: 1.9%*

Black persons: 1.2%*

American Indian and Alaska Native persons: 0.3%*

Native Hawaiian and Other Pacific Islanders: 0.04%*

Persons reporting two or more races: 1.0%

Persons of Hispanic or Latino origin: 2.5%†

White persons not Hispanic: 93.4%

Includes persons reporting only one race.
† Hispanics may be of any race, so they are also included in applicable race categories.

Weather

Record high temperature 106°F (41°C) at Nashua on July 4, 1911
Record low temperature −47°F (−44°C) at Mount Washington on January 29, 1934
Average July temperature 71°F (22°C)
Average January temperature 23°F (−5°C)
Average yearly precipitation 37 inches (94 cm)

State flag

STATE SONG

★ ★ ★

"Old New Hampshire"

New Hampshire's state song was written in 1926 and adopted as the official state song in 1949. The words are by John F. Holmes, and the music is by Maurice Hoffmann.

With a skill that knows no measure
From the golden store of fate
God, in His great love and wisdom,
Made the rugged Granite State;
Made the lakes, the fields, the forests;
Made the rivers and the rills;
Made the bubbling, crystal fountains
Of New Hampshire's Granite Hills.

Chorus
Old New Hampshire, Old New Hampshire
Old New Hampshire grand and great
We will sing of Old New Hampshire
Of the dear old Granite State.

Builded he New Hampshire glorious
From the borders to the sea
And with matchless charm and splendor
Blessed her for eternity.
Hers, the majesty of mountains;
Hers, the grandeur of the lake;
Hers, the truth as from the hillside
Whence her crystal waters break.

(Chorus)

NATURAL AREAS AND HISTORIC SITES

National Scenic Trail

About 150 miles (241 km) of the 2,174-mile (3,499 km) *Appalachian National Scenic Trail* pass through New Hampshire, traversing the state's rugged hills and valleys.

National Historic Site

Saint-Gaudens National Historic Site, New Hampshire's only national historic site, is one of only two sites in the national park system dedicated to a visual artist. It includes the home, studios, and gardens of the sculptor Augustus Saint-Gaudens.

National Forest

New Hampshire's *White Mountain National Forest* is in the White Mountains Region of the state. More than 100 miles (161 km) of the Appalachian National Scenic Trail pass through this forest.

State Parks and Forests

New Hampshire's state park system features and maintains 68 state parks and recreation areas, including *Bear Brook State Park*, which is one of New Hampshire's largest state parks; *Jericho Lake State Park*; *Miller State Park*, which is the oldest state-run park in New Hampshire; and *Mount Washington State Park*, which is located up on the summit of Mount Washington, the highest point in the Northeast.

Backpacking in White Mountain National Forest

SPORTS TEAMS

★ ★ ★

NCAA Teams (Division I)

Dartmouth College *Big Green*
University of New Hampshire *Wildcats*

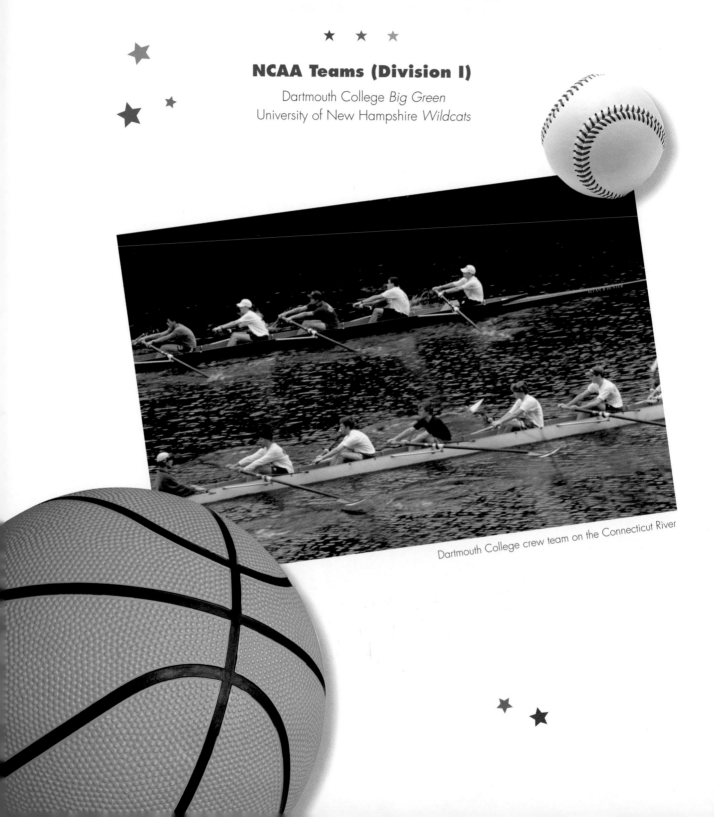

Dartmouth College crew team on the Connecticut River

CULTURAL INSTITUTIONS

Libraries

Baker Library at Dartmouth College (Hanover) contains an impressive collection of original manuscripts by writers such as Joseph Conrad, Robert Burns, and Herman Melville.

Portsmouth Athenaeum (Portsmouth), one of the oldest membership libraries in the United States, contains important collections of local historical manuscripts, as well as ship models, paintings, and other artifacts.

Museums

The *Currier Museum of Art* (Manchester) holds the state's finest collection of paintings, including many notable works by important U.S. and European artists.

Hood Museum of Art (Hanover) houses a fine collection of art at the Dartmouth College campus.

The *New Hampshire Historical Society* (Concord) contains interesting period rooms and collections of materials related to the state's history.

Mount Kearsarge Indian Museum (Warner) has exhibits and demonstrations about the lifeways and culture of the Native Americans of New Hampshire.

Seacoast African American Cultural Center (Portsmouth) brings to life African American history in early New Hampshire, emphasizing the people of the Seacoast community.

Performing Arts

New Hampshire has one major opera company.

Universities and Colleges

In 2006, New Hampshire had nine public and 14 private institutions of higher learning.

ANNUAL EVENTS

January–March

Winter Carnivals in Franconia, Hanover, Lincoln, and Plymouth (January and February)

Annual World Championship Sled Dog Derby in Laconia (February)

April–June

Celtic Crossroads Festival in Lincoln (May)

Sheep and Wool Festival in New Boston (May)

Lilac Festival Parade in Lisbon (May)

Stark Fiddlers' Contest in Stark (June)

Market Square Day Celebration in Portsmouth (June)

July–September

Prescott Parks Art Festival in Portsmouth (July and August)

Carved pumpkins at the Pumpkin Festival in Keene

Pemi Valley Bluegrass Festival in Campton (August)

League of New Hampshire Craftsmen's Fair in Mount Sunapee State Park (August)

Rubber Ducky Regatta in North Woodstock (September)

Riverfest Celebration in Manchester (September)

Highland Games at Loon Mountain in Lincoln (September)

October–December

Fall Foliage Tour in Charlestown (October)

Sandwich Fair (October)

Pumpkin Festival in Keene (October)

Candlelight Stroll at Strawbery Banke in Portsmouth (December)

First Night New Hampshire in Concord, Keene, Portsmouth, and Wolfeboro (December 31)

Sarah Bagley (1806–1883) was the first woman in the United States to establish a trade union. She was from Candia.

Josiah Bartlett (1729–1795) signed the Declaration of Independence and served as New Hampshire's first governor.

Amy Beach See page 81.

Laura Bridgman See page 77.

Alice Brown (1856–1948) wrote short stories and plays about New England life. Her best-known plays are *Children of Earth* and *Meadow-Grass*.

Dan Brown (1964–) is the author of the 2004 best-seller *The Da Vinci Code*, a fast-paced novel of intrigue. He was born in Exeter.

Ken Burns (1953–) is a documentary filmmaker who uses many photographs and original documents in his work, such as the TV miniseries *Jazz*, *Baseball*, and *The Civil War*. He lives in Walpole.

David Carroll See page 21.

William E. Chandler (1835–1917) of Concord was an outspoken newspaper editor during the 1870s. He served as secretary of the navy under President Chester Arthur and assistant secretary of the treasury under President Andrew Johnson. He was elected to the U.S. Senate in 1887 and served until 1901.

Ken Burns

Salmon P. Chase (1808–1873) served as secretary of the treasury and chief justice of the U.S. Supreme Court under Abraham Lincoln. He was born in Cornish and attended Dartmouth College.

Winston Churchill (1871–1947) served in the state legislature and wrote many books about his home state. His novel *Coniston* drew upon his experience in the legislature and exposed corruption in New Hampshire's government.

Robin Cook

Eunice Cole (1590?–1680?) was the only person ever convicted of witchcraft in colonial New Hampshire. She spent 15 years in prison.

Thomas Cole (1801–1848) was an American landscape painter. He is best known for paintings of New York's Hudson River valley, but he also painted images of the White Mountains such as *View of Mount Washington* and *View near Conway*.

Robin Cook (1940–), who spends summers in Waterville Valley, is the author of many popular medical thrillers including *Coma* and *Toxin*. He is a practicing physician.

Harriet Dame See page 54.

Charles A. Dana (1819–1897) was a journalist and newspaper editor who was born in Hinsdale. As editor of the *New York Sun*, he actively worked to end slavery and later became a strong supporter of the Union during the Civil War.

Tomie dePaola (1934–) is an author and illustrator of books for children. He won a Caldecott Honor Award for *Strega Nona* and a Newbery Honor Award for *26 Fairmount Avenue*. He lives and works in New London.

Hannah Duston (1657–1736) became a legend of the New England frontier. She and two family servants were captured by Native Americans in Massachusetts. They then set off for Canada, where she and the others were to become slaves. On the way, Duston killed her captors, including several Indian children, and made her escape.

Mary Baker Eddy (1821–1910) founded the Christian Science Church, which is based on the idea that prayer can lead to the healing of disease. She was born and raised in Bow.

Carlton Fisk (1947–), from Charlestown, is an all-star baseball player who played catcher for the Boston Red Sox and the Chicago White Sox for a total of 24 years. He was elected to the National Baseball Hall of Fame in 2000.

Mike Flanagan (1951–) is a Major League Baseball pitcher who spent most of his career with the Baltimore Orioles. He won the Cy Young Award for best pitcher of the year in 1979. He is from Manchester.

Carlton Fisk

Elizabeth Gurley Flynn (1890–1964) helped found the American Civil Liberties Union, an organization that works to protect the constitutional rights of Americans. She lived in Concord until the age of 10, when her family moved to New York.

Stephen Symonds Foster (1809–1881) was a preacher and antislavery activist from Hanover, who was known for his fiery speeches. He helped establish the New Hampshire Antislavery Society and published a book against slavery called *The Brotherhood of Thieves* (1843).

Daniel Chester French (1850–1931) was a sculptor who made the statue of Abraham Lincoln for the Lincoln Memorial in Washington, D.C. He was born in Exeter.

Robert Frost (1874–1963), who spent much of his life in Derry and Franconia, is considered one of America's leading poets. He wrote about New Hampshire farm life in poems such as "Mending Wall" and "The Death of the Hired Man."

Horace Greeley (1811–1872) was a New York congressman and publisher of the *New York Tribune*. During the era when the country was expanding westward, he encouraged people with the words, "Go west, young man!" He was born in Amherst.

Sarah Josepha Hale (1788–1879), who was born in Newport, edited a popular magazine called *Godey's Lady's Book* and wrote the nursery rhyme "Mary Had a Little Lamb." She was the most influential female editor in the United States during the 19th century.

Sarah Josepha Hale

Donald Hall (1928–) is a noted poet and memoirist who settled on a New Hampshire farm in 1975. The New Hampshire setting inspired works such as *Seasons at Eagle Pond* and *Life Work*.

Otto (1915–) and **Vivika (1910–1995) Heino** worked together as potters and taught at the League of New Hampshire Craftsmen during the 1950s.

John Irving (1942–) is a novelist who attended Exeter and the University of New Hampshire. His books include *The World According to Garp* and *The Cider House Rules*.

Lotte Jacobi (1896–1990) was a German-born photographer who worked for *Life* magazine in the 1950s. She took candid photos of famous people including Albert Einstein, Robert Frost, and Eleanor Roosevelt. She settled in Deering in 1960.

Dean Kamen See page 102.

Jane Kenyon (1947–1995) was a poet from Michigan whose collections include *From Room to Room*, *Let Evening Come*, and *Constance*. She married poet Donald Hall in 1972 and moved with him to his farm at Eagle Pond. She was New Hampshire's poet laureate at the time of her death.

Mandy Moore

Maxine Kumin (1925–) is a poet, essayist, and novelist. Among her books are the poetry collections *The Nightmare Factory* and *Looking for Luck*, and the novels *The Abduction* and *The Designated Heir*. She lives on a farm near Warner.

Edward MacDowell (1860–1908) was a composer and pianist. He and his wife, Marian, founded the MacDowell Colony, a retreat for artists in Peterborough.

Omer Marcoux (1898–1982) was a French Canadian musician who moved to Concord in the mid-1920s. He became one of the nation's best-known French-New England fiddlers with "Face Me Up" and other reels.

Christa McAuliffe See page 66.

Seth Meyers (1973–) is a comedian and actor who is the lead writer on the TV show *Saturday Night Live*. He was born and raised in Bedford.

Bode Miller

Bode Miller (1977–) is a World Cup champion skier. He was born in Easton and teaches skiing at Bretton Woods.

Bob Montana (1920–1975) was a popular cartoonist. He based his long-running comic strip *Archie* on his high school experiences in Manchester.

Mandy Moore (1984–) is a singer, songwriter, actor, model, and fashion designer who was born in Nashua. She has appeared in movies including *A Walk to Remember* and *The Princess Diaries*.

Samson Occom (1723–1792), who belonged to the Mohegan Nation of Connecticut, became a Christian minister and worked among the Native Americans of New England. He spent nearly two years in England raising money to help found Dartmouth College for the education of Indian and English youth.

Maxfield Parrish (1870–1966) illustrated children's books and advertisements. He spent most of his working life in Cornish.

Passaconaway See page 38.

Jodi Picoult (1966–) is a novelist who lives and writes in Hanover. Her books, which often focus on people wrestling with ethical issues, include *Songs of the Humpback Whale*, *Mercy*, and *Nineteen Minutes*.

Franklin Pierce See page 94.

Eleanor Hodgman Porter See page 82.

Richard Potter (1783–1835) is considered the first successful American stage magician. He had an English father and an African American mother, and lived in Hopkinton.

Abraham Prescott (1789–1858) was a renowned instrument maker whose double basses remain highly prized by musicians today. He worked in Deerfield and Concord.

Robert Rogers See page 40.

Augustus Saint-Gaudens (1848–1907) was a sculptor who created figures of Civil War generals and reliefs of scenes from U.S. history. In his final years, he settled in Cornish, where he became the center of a community of artists and writers.

J. D. Salinger (1919–) is a reclusive writer whose works include the classic novel *The Catcher in the Rye*, about a teenager disenchanted with the world. He has lived in Cornish since 1953.

Adam Sandler

Adam Sandler (1966–) is an actor who starred in films such as *Happy Gilmore*, *Big Daddy*, and *Spanglish*. He grew up in Manchester.

Jeanne Shaheen

Jeanne Shaheen (1947–) was born in Missouri and moved to New Hampshire in 1973. She taught school and ran a small business, but her passion was for politics. In 1990, she was elected to the New Hampshire Senate, and in 1996 she became the Granite State's first female governor. In 2008, she was elected to the U.S. Senate.

Alan Shepard Jr. (1923–1998) of Derry was an astronaut. In 1961, he became the first American to go into space. Ten years later, he became the fifth astronaut to walk on the moon.

David Souter See page 93.

John Stark See page 44.

John H. Sununu (1939–) served as governor of New Hampshire from 1983 to 1989 and was the White House chief of staff for President George H. W. Bush from 1989 to 1992. He was born in Havana, Cuba.

Celia Laighton Thaxter (1835–1894) was a popular poet who wrote about the Isles of Shoals and the New Hampshire seacoast.

Jenny Thompson See page 85.

Earl Silas Tupper (1907–1983) invented the airtight plastic storage containers called Tupperware. He grew up on a farm near Berlin.

Daniel Webster See page 53.

John Gilbert Winant (1889–1947) was a four-term governor of New Hampshire and ambassador to Great Britain. During the Great Depression, he developed a variety of programs to help New Hampshire's unemployed.

RESOURCES

★ ★ ★

BOOKS

Nonfiction

Caravantes, Peggy. *Deep Woods: The Story of Robert Frost*. Greensboro, N.C.: Morgan Reynolds, 2006.

Gray, Susan H. *Karner Blue Butterfly*. Ann Arbor, Mich.: Cherry Lake Publishing, 2007.

Harvey, Bonnie C. *Daniel Webster: Liberty and Union, Now and Forever*. Berkeley Heights, N.J.: Enslow, 2001.

Haulley, Fletcher. *A Primary Source History of the Colony of New Hampshire*. New York: Rosen, 2006.

Michelson, Richard. *Tuttle's Red Barn: The Story of America's Oldest Family Farm*. New York: G. P. Putnam, 2006.

Venezia, Mike. *Franklin Pierce*. New York: Children's Press, 2005.

Fiction

Banks, Kate. *Dillon Dillon*. New York: Frances Foster/Farrar, Straus and Giroux, 2002.

Harrar, George. *The Trouble with Jeremy Chance*. Minneapolis: Milkweed Editions, 2003.

Schmidt, Gary D. *First Boy*. New York: Henry Holt, 2005.

DVDs

Discoveries . . . America: New Hampshire. Bennett-Watt Entertainment, 2004.

Nightline UpClose: Dean Kamen. ABC News, 2007.

Our Town. PBS Pictures, 2003.

Rivers of North America: Connecticut River. Film Ideas, Inc., 2008.

WEB SITES AND ORGANIZATIONS

Canterbury Shaker Village

www.shakers.org

To learn more about this national historic landmark and museum.

New Hampshire Almanac

www.nh.gov/nhinfo

To find material about New Hampshire's geography, history, and government.

New Hampshire Division of Parks and Recreation

www.nhparks.state.nh.us

For a list of state parks, visitor guidelines, and information about historic sites.

New Hampshire Historical Society

www.nhhistory.org

This site gives information about the programs and resources available through the society museum.

New Hampshire State Government

www.nh.gov

For information about how the state government works and who the leaders are.

New Hampshire Timeline of State History

www.shgresources.com/nh/timeline

For a chronological history of New Hampshire and information about state symbols.

Seacoast New Hampshire

www.seacoastNH.com

For links to information on the history and attractions of New Hampshire's seacoast.

Welcome to New Hampshire

www.visitnh.gov

For vacation information and advice on great places to visit.

INDEX

★ ★ ★

AUTHOR'S TIPS AND SOURCE NOTES

★   ★   ★

Several books on New Hampshire proved valuable in my research for this book. *New Hampshire: An Illustrated History of the Granite State* by Ronald Jager and Grace Jager was both informative and a pleasure to read. Other helpful books were *The Indian Heritage of New Hampshire and Northern New England* edited by Thaddeus Piotrowski and *New Hampshire: A Bicentennial History* by Elizabeth Forbes Morison and Elting Morison. Useful Web sites included those of the New Hampshire Historical Society (www.nhhistory.org) and the New Hampshire Almanac (www.nh.gov/nhinfo).